Praise for *Heartbeat of a Survivor*

Wow. What a life.... Nita's Tin story is truly hard to believe, and she has captured it so well in these pages. From Burma to New York to Chattanooga, from wealth to poverty and everything in between, Nita and her amazing husband faced challenges you will struggle to believe. Nita Tin is a courageous survivor who lives out the word 'grace' like no one we have ever met. One of the riches blessings of Sharon and I moving to Georgia has been meeting and getting to know Nita and her lovely daughter, Mimi. This book needs to be a Television Series!!!!
– Mark Fincannon, CSA: Casting Director

How to find the words to describe Nita Tin and the story she's lived? Exotic, dangerous, romantic, spiritual, and mysterious might explain a portion of her story, but, oh, there is so much more because her life is God's story. It will draw you in, leave you with insights for your own life, and give you hope that the God who wrote such an amazing story for Nita Tin and her family can write a unique, purposeful story for you.
– Jan Silvous, Author, Speaker, Life Coach

Nita Tin has always walked with the Lord, depended on Him, and desired to glorify Him in everything she does. She knows the reason she has written her story, *Heartbeat of a Survivor*. It's not to be popular or to receive accolades but to be an ambassador for Jesus Christ. God sent Nita as an example among believers in thought, word, and deed, and in purity, godliness, and holiness—and it is a privilege to say these things. She is a valiant warrior. God has given her to us as a representative of what He will do when we walk fully hand in hand with the Lord, desiring to serve Him and exalt Him as we take no glory for ourselves.
– Kay Arthur, Author, Speaker, Bible teacher

Nita Tin's story seems like something that couldn't have really happened, but it did—the wealth, the poverty; the darkness, the light; the way she and her husband have loved each other; and the way they have loved God. I often wondered, *Did they really love each other and trust God like that?* Yes, they did. But don't believe me. Read for yourself.

– **Peter Lundell**, *Author, Editor, Pastor*

Nita Tin's story shares God's love and faithfulness through her darkest and most challenging times. As she finds the love of her life, she also discovers a joy and love that surpasses all understanding in her Heavenly Father. As you read Nita's story, you will experience God's grace, mercy, and redemption in *Heartbeat of a Survivor*. It is a journey of perseverance and transformation. I have no doubt that you will draw great inspiration for your own life through Nita's memoir. It is an adventure like no other, and I can't wait to see it on the Big Screen.

– **Lisa Arnold**, *Director, Writer, Producer*

It is hard to find a sweeter soul than Nita Tin. Her heart has been shaped by the loving faithfulness of our God who pursued her for His honor and glory. Nita's tender smile and kind reminders of God's love amaze so many as they realize the heartaches and struggles that she endured. Her story reminds us that God strengthens, heals, and restores those who wholeheartedly depend on Him.

– **Melanie Lewis**, *Biblical Church Counselor*

One family's remarkable adventure following a sovereign God... Be inspired by this courageous family in the captivating story of survival and of flourishing in a new land of boundless opportunities as told by Nita Tin, a godly woman of honor.

– **Dan T. Cathy**, *Visionary, Town at Trilith and Trilith Studios*

HEARTBEAT
OF A
SURVIVOR

FROM GOLDEN PAGODAS TO A SOUL SET FREE

A True Story by NITA TIN

Heartbeat of a Survivor: From Golden Pagodas to a Soul Set Free
Copyright © 2023 Nita Tin
Cover Art by Mimi Tin

World Publishing and Productions
PO Box 8722, Jupiter, FL 33468
worldpublishingandproductions.com

ISBN: 978-1-957111-22-3
Library of Congress Control Number: 2023920015

Scripture quotations noted as AMP are taken from The Amplified Bible®, Copyright © 1965, 1987, 2015 by The Lockman Foundation. All rights reserved. Used by permission. (www.Lockman.org).

Scripture quotations noted as KJV are taken from the King James Version of the Bible, public domain.

Scripture quotations noted as NASB are taken from the New American Standard Bible, © 1960, 1962, 1963, 1968, 1971, 1972, 1973, 1975, 1977, 1995, 2020 by The Lockman Foundation. Used by permission.

Scripture quotations noted as NIV are taken from the Holy Bible, New International Version® NIV®. Copyright © 1973, 1978, 1984, 2011 by the International Bible Society. Used by permission of Zondervan Publishing House. All rights reserved worldwide.

Scripture quotations noted as MSG are taken from *The Message*. Copyright © 1993, 1994, 1995, 1996, 2000, 2001, 2002. Used by permission of NavPress Publishing Group.

To My Forever Husband,
My soulmate, the one whom our Lord gifted me with.

I was barely sixteen, and you were not yet twenty
when God brought you into my life and changed me forever.
Love of my life, through your life, I understood;
your Maker became mine; your God became my God.
As hands outstretched, I took the gift of pardon
so freely offered without ties,
unspeakable joy as you introduced me to your Savior,
and He became my Savior, too.
One faith, one love, one hope, one joy,
no longer separated, we became one in His love.

Contents

Acknowledgments

To my ageless, joyful, drive-me-crazy, creative graphic designer daughter, Mimi Tin (mimitin.com), who hounded me into starting my book and kept on until I finished it, and to my gentle, quiet, laid-back physician son, who has cheered me on behind the scenes: I love you both.

To Melanie Lewis, Biblical Church Counselor and co-founder of Desperately Dependent Community (ddcommunity.org), who lovingly challenged me not to die without leaving the legacy of my story behind: my grateful thanks.

To Kay Arthur, Author, Speaker, Co-founder and Bible teacher of Precept Ministries International (precept.org), who has grounded me in the Word of God and mentored me for more than fifty years: I am deeply indebted to you.

To my coaches—Jan Silvious, Author, Speaker, Life Coach (jansilvious.com); Jerry Jenkins, Author, and his team at Jerry Jenkins Guild (jerryjenkins.com); and Debra Englander on Steve Harrison's team (steveharrison.com): you have taught me so much about the art of writing.

To my nephew, John Doliner, and my long-time friend, Susan Simmons, who read my drafts and entire manuscript and gave me valuable feedback: I salute you both.

To all the people I taught in Bible study for over forty years and those who listened to me speak: you gave me the platform to dig deep into the Scriptures and expanded my mind in countless ways.

To Lisa Arnold (checkthegateproductions.com), who wrote the film script for *Love Without Borders* based on my book *Heartbeat of a Survivor* and introduced me to Kimberly Hobbs and Julie Jenkins (womenworldle aders.com & worldpublishingandproductions.com), who perfected and published my book. My heartfelt thanks go to all three of you.

To Rhonda and Dan Cathy (Visionary for Town at Trilith and Trilith Studios), who welcomed me to this beautiful neighborhood built for creatives where I was inspired to finish my book: my sincere thanks.

To the many people who stood with me in prayer, especially Sharon and Mark Fincannon (fincannoncasting.com), who introduced me to the person who would walk the last lap with me in writing my story: I thank you all.

And finally, but most importantly, I owe a debt of gratitude to Peter Lundell, Author and Editor (peterlundell.com), for tirelessly and painstakingly editing my manuscript and helping bring this memoir to life and excellence.

Preface

I am passionate about sharing this story because I was the person who was set free from bondage, fear, and tyranny to a life overflowing with freedom, joy, and love.

Through the valleys and difficult trials in my life, I discovered that no matter the circumstance, pain, heartache, loss, or sorrow, God can break the chains that hold us, leading us to a life that is abundant and meaningful.

My story is a faith journey of unending marital romance rooted in a never-ending spiritual hunger and an ever-growing experience of God's love.

Part I

In Search of Something More

Chapter 1

"Shh, Don't Look Behind You"

Without dark clouds in our lives,
we would never know the joy of sunshine.
We can become callous and unteachable
if we do not learn from pain.
–Billy Graham[1]

November 2, 1973, Rangoon, Burma (now Myanmar)

That pivotal day arrived—after two long years of waiting for the government to release our passports so we could leave our native land, our *home*. The waiting had taken its toll. Now we were close to the last hurdle.

The telephone shrilled. Hands shaking, I lifted the receiver to my ear. The line crackled, and a female voice said, "You need to come now. Don't delay. The officer will see you at 3:30 p.m."

My husband turned. "If we hurry, we can make it on time."

We arrived at the customs office, where an unsmiling officer greeted us coldly. "Your passports have been stamped by the American Consulate for entry into the US, but you will have to sign these papers before they are released to you. Leaving is an act of treason."

He continued in a detached monotone. "You will also have to pay the government five years' income tax in advance as well as ten thousand kyats each. The equivalent, as given by the bank today, is seven kyats to the US dollar. You will not be allowed to take any jewelry or photographs with you."

He did not look at us. "I will be back in ten minutes. Have the papers signed and the cash ready. You will not get your departure forms or your permission forms until all the requirements are carried out."

He turned and strode out of the room.

This Is the Only Way

My husband picked up the papers the security officer left on the table. "Just look at this! It says that we are admitting to being traitors to our country. We cannot sign this."

I motioned to the tiny microphone on the desk. Our freedom of speech was gone, and anything we said that was contrary to the socialist republic was punishable. We were so close to the brink of getting to leave. I put my trembling hand on his. "We must sign the papers. This is the only way."

Ten minutes later, the security officer strode in. He took the papers and laid the four passports and the departure and permission forms on the table. "You are allowed to take twenty dollars out of the country," he said mechanically. "The departure forms and the permission forms will be stamped by the bank executive when you have paid the required amount. The bank is closing at 4 p.m. You have fifteen minutes. Go to the one down this corridor. If you don't make it to the bank executive in time, you will have to return in the morning."

Panic seized us. It was 3:45 p.m. The airline tickets we had rebooked were cleared for 7 p.m. that night.

"Hurry, Darling. We have no time to lose." With the departure forms, permission forms, and four stamped passports in hand, we rushed over to the government bank to pay the five years' tax, the twenty thousand kyat fine, and the equivalent of twenty dollars. The bank executive was a longtime friend of the family and my husband's classmate.

He received the items, and in turn, he handed Pe a twenty-dollar bill without a smile. "This is what you are allowed to leave the country with." He stamped the government seal on the departure and permission forms, put them in an envelope, and gave it to Pe without looking at either of us. He was also being watched.

We sped hurriedly across the quadrangle where we had left my husband's jeep. Our small luggage had been packed for immediate departure. Our children were at my parents' house and would be ready and waiting for us to pick them up.

As we drove out of the parking lot, I took a deep breath. "Darling, I'm just now trying to wrap my head around the finality of leaving our beloved country, but now that it is ruled by the military dictator, our decision is for the best." I hesitated. "You do think so, don't you?"

He turned his oh-so-dear and familiar face to me but didn't answer.

I searched his face but couldn't tell his thoughts. I sensed he was waiting for me to process my jumbled thoughts. He knew me so well. My brain was spinning. "Waiting for two years until this point has been exhausting with so many roadblocks and red tape hindering us at every turn, and this final week has been so tense. My mind has been alternating between despair and hope."

I moved closer to him, drawing strength from him. "My emotions have been raw. It has been a big decision, and I'm glad you made it for us. It's going to be better for our babies, and like you said, this is no longer a desirable place for them to grow up."

Pe's soft and gentle eyes brimmed over. He nodded. He did not need to say anything. He picked up my hand and kissed my ring finger. My wedding ring was inscribed with the words, *Forever Yours 4th March 1967*. It would be left behind. As would my twin pearl and diamond engagement ring that was his mother's and the sapphire and ruby gold bangles my grandmothers had given me.

The previous night, before Pe switched off the bedside lamp, I quietly whispered so the children would not hear, "I hope they call us. I am so worried. We need to get our papers so we can catch the flight out tomorrow." Then I tossed and turned all night, trying to sleep.

We had gotten up early, rubbing our eyes for lack of sleep, and the rest of the day was a blur. We went through the motions almost like zombies as we waited for the call from the customs office.

Now, with our papers and passports and the precious twenty-dollar bill, we rushed to my parents' home to pick up our children. My tired mind finally grasped that we had been granted permission to leave Burma. I pinched myself and gently touched my husband's hand, placed firmly on the steering wheel. He reached out and warmly held my hand in his, comforting me.

Feelings of relief flooded my anxious heart, but they only lasted a moment. It suddenly hit me that we would be leaving our home, including our family, friends, savings, and everything we owned. Within hours, we would surrender my engagement and wedding rings, jewelry, photographs, and all we cherished. Pe gripped my shaky hand and whispered, "It's going to be all right. God will take care of us."

We Will See You Again

Our parents and my sisters were at their front door when we arrived. Hugging them close, I whispered, "It is time. We've been released, and we must go. We must leave immediately." My voice quivered as I bravely told them, "We love you so much."

Pe drew all of us into a circle, bowed his head, and prayed to God, giving thanks. Then, with our hands clasped around each other's waists, a strange peace settled on us all, filling me with the hope that we would all see each other again one day.

"We love you," Mum whispered, teary-eyed. "We will be praying for your safety."

"We haven't told anyone," Daddy added. I knew the unannounced arrest and immediate imprisonment by the government moments before he was to leave for Australia was heavy on his mind.

Tears ran down my cheeks as I unzipped my travel handbag, tucking away our passports and the twenty-dollar bill into a safe compartment. The letter from the US Consulate, the airline tickets, and the Social Security Cards for all four of us were already in that file pocket. Resolutely, I zipped up the bag.

I looked at the hallway clock and picked up my handbag in silence. While Pe carried our daughter and the small suitcase, I held our son's hand. Then, with Pe's father, my parents, and my sisters coming to see us off, Daddy's two chauffeurs drove us all in two separate cars to the Rangoon airport.

It was just past dusk. We were driving down the road, and I had an uncanny feeling that we were being watched.

Uppermost in my mind was the dreadful memory from six months earlier, when Daddy was stopped on what was to be the eve of my parents' departure to Australia. The authorities confiscated his passport and then relentlessly tortured and questioned him. Then, beaten and powerless, he was locked up. Although Daddy's London office secured his release by paying his ransom, he was told that he and my mother and sisters would be detained for a year. My family's desire to begin a life unhampered by the Burmese socialist military regime abruptly collapsed around them. Pe and I certainly did not want a similar outcome.

The road to the airport stretched longer than usual. The night was eerie, and our senses were on alert as we drove beneath the ominous stillness of the trees lining the darkened street. Shadows chased each other as several pairs of headlights appeared behind us.

"Are we being followed? Those three cars behind us are close on our tail."

Pe whispered in my ear, "I don't know. Just keep on praying."

Dark clouds had gathered as we left my parents' home, but now we could hear a few sounds of thunder. A flash of lightning brightened the skies, and the heavens broke loose with a heavy downpour. Still, the headlights followed and seemed to loom even closer.

We approached the airport gate and saw a lineup of guards with loaded automatic rifles.

"I need to see your documents." The security guard stopped us, holding out his gloved hand. He stared intently at each of us, then looked closely at the papers we presented. Finally, after what seemed hours, he barked out some orders and waved his hand in a gesture of dismissal, sweeping us through the barricade.

I was trembling now. Pe held me close. Feelings of fear and trepidation, coupled with the thought that we might never see our families again, imprisoned me in a vise-like grip. The unknown stretched in front of me, and it was all I could do to chase those frightening thoughts away. "It's alright, Darling. God has already gone ahead of us. He will never leave us."

Our two cars stopped at the curb, and we all got out. We said goodbye to our families, holding tightly to each embrace, which seemed more precious than the last. Then, with tears in our eyes, we stood waving from the doorway as they drove away—bravely harnessing our resolve—until we could not see them anymore. Apprehensively, Pe and I, each carrying a child on one arm and our small bags with the other, walked toward the line cordoned off for security screening and departure.

Will They Let Us Go?

Our turn came, and the children and I passed through security. But when I looked behind me, I saw that Pe was being detained. He was being questioned heavily. Although I couldn't understand the precise words, I did hear his brother's name mentioned. Then, more photographs were taken, and another confession had to be signed. They searched Pe's whole body, from head to toe, as I watched transfixed. I felt as though I had stopped breathing as I stood waiting resolutely with my children.

When I finally saw the hand that waved him through, I heaved a sigh of relief. Pe quietly joined us on the other side of the security barricade and softly held my arm.

As he quickly bent down to hug all three of us, our five-year-old son whispered, "Are they going to let us go?"

Pent-up emotions flooded Pe and me as we both whispered back in unison, "We don't know yet."

Soon we were at the customs line. They searched our small bags. Having left everything behind, we passed through customs with nothing to declare.

As we sat in the waiting room, anxiously prepared to be called for boarding, I glanced back. Two men in military uniform had followed us all through the airport and were now seated behind us. I noticed a revolver in the hip pocket of one of the men; they had an air about them that I could not put my finger on. I quickly turned back around. Still, I could feel them moving closer to us.

I put a restraining hand on Pe's arm. "Shhh, don't look behind you."

With bated breath, we started walking quickly toward the gate where they were announcing that the British Airways jet we were taking had landed. As we hurriedly joined the line now forming, the two men followed closely.

"Will they let us go?" I whispered.

"Keep on moving." He reached out to hold my shaking hand.

Chapter 2

Déjà vu in Kathmandu

How beautiful on the mountains
are the feet of those who bring good news,
who proclaim peace,
who bring good tidings,
who proclaim salvation,
who say to Zion, "Your God reigns."
–Isaiah 52:7 NIV

February 7, 2014, Nepal

Forty-one years after that fateful night at Rangoon Airport, a gust of cold wind whipped the faces of a group of Americans as they stepped out from the airport shuttle in Kathmandu, Nepal. Pe, our daughter Mimi, and I were part of the group of men and women who had come to participate in a conference that was a life-changing experience for me. The teaching sessions were now over, and we had been promised that this part of our itinerary would be the most momentous, jaw-dropping adventure of our lives.

Once we were in the airport, a voice in Nepalese, followed by a translation in English, came over the speakers, "All passengers taking the tour to Mt. Everest, please form a line at the counter and please enter the plane."

There, cruising in on the tarmac, was a high-wing Fokker Friendship plane proudly sporting the name *Buddha Airlines*. My heart thumped at the thought of cruising in a chartered plane above Mt. Everest, 29,002 feet above sea level.

"Look, Darling, look!" Pe said as he took the seat across the aisle from me. Mimi was in the row behind me. "We each get a whole row! Can't wait to use my new camera."

Click, click, click—the sound of seat belts being fastened, the varying cadences of cell phones and laptops being turned off, and the musical voice of the air hostess giving last-minute instructions heralded the start of our amazing journey into the sky.

As the plane made the ascent into the cloudless blue sky, I settled into my seat and closed my eyes in quiet reverie. My mind went back to the beginning of the week when thirty Americans had crossed the oceans to minister to the more than 1200 Nepalese students gathered in Kathmandu for the conference that was planned to encourage and strengthen them.

Only a month earlier, the president of this global ministry had invited me to come. "I know this request is somewhat of a surprise and does not give you much time to get ready, but I know that as a Burmese woman brought up in a Buddhist-Hindu culture, you will be able to minister to them."

His voice was passionate.

"These church planters are people with beautiful feet, carrying the good news all over the mountains of Nepal. We have been given the opportunity to meet these nationals right where they are—to teach, train, uplift, and encourage them. The crowning moment of this much-prayed-for symposium will be for us to wash each individual church planter's feet and to bow over their heads and pray for them."

Pe and Mimi had wholeheartedly agreed to accompany me. So we put our work on hold for this journey that had seemingly come from nowhere, and now we were all here in Kathmandu, joining hands with people we did not know to work on a project we were not familiar with. We had been working non-stop on this teaching and training trip, and this trip to the Himalayas was a welcome reprieve.

Unbidden, a heartbreaking scene flashed across my mind from a couple of days earlier when we had visited a Hindu cemetery. A woman's body had been left burning on a funeral pyre along a dirty, muddy river. A woman was crying nearby. "Lady, is that your mother?" I asked her.

"Yes," she nodded. "It is our custom. We believe that her ashes will float into eternity." Such faith! Such sincerity! I was deeply touched.

This brought another scene to mind. We had gone on to visit a Buddhist monastery and a nearby temple. There, a woman had been splashing her head and body with holy water where she had sacrificed meat to the monkey god, hoping he would cleanse her. Shivering with the recollection, I was thankful I had escaped from the neighboring country of Burma, now known as Myanmar, and no longer lived in fear and bondage to the things I had once worshipped yet never satisfied my seeking heart.

Had I come to another crossroads in my life? Would there be another sign? Would there be another big change?

I began to ask myself if there was a reason I had been brought back to Eastern culture. What difference could my insignificant life make? While packing my bags in haste the night before I left for Nepal (because, as usual, I had left it to the last minute), I had asked myself those same questions that begged for answers not yet revealed to me.

No More Shackles

"Are you okay, Darling?" Pe had slipped into the seat beside me and held my hand tightly.

"Yes, it was just that those dreams came back, and I think it's because Nepal is so close to Burma. Being in those places brought back the old memories of when I was so scared to go into the Hindu temple to pray with Daddy's mother. I must have been about eight years old then, but to this day, I can still smell the overpowering incense and all the ripening fruit left as an offering."

"It's all right, my Darling. Try not to think about it." He put his arm around me and pulled me closer to his side.

"Yes, I know," I was trying hard to shake the unwanted, unbidden memories circulating in my brain. "I was also thinking about the times I would go to the Buddhist monastery with Mummy's mother. That didn't scare me, but I always felt so hopeless and empty."

Pe held me closer and smoothed my forehead. "We're together now. It is all in the past."

The plane leveled, and we were now cruising. Range after mountain range came up to meet row upon row of eyes, round and bright with awe and wonder. I took in the scene. The passengers, now allowed out of their seats, clambered across aisles, took turns going into the cockpit, and crowded to one side or the other to capture the best view.

Snuggled in my corner seat with Pe sitting next to me, I looked out the window and saw flags dotted here and there, marking the places where brave people had conquered hitherto unconquerable majestic slopes.

This amazing plane ride with people moving about would have seemed bizarre to the average traveler. But to me, it spoke volumes. Before I could share my thoughts, Pe turned his face to mine.

"This freedom of being able to go in and out of the cockpit makes me think of Hebrews 4:16. It is amazing that we have been set free and can boldly enter the throne room of grace at any point of our need." He shook his head in wonderment. "No more shackles! Our loving God has set the captives free and opened the entrance into the Holy of Holies! How amazing is that?"

You Can Always Make a U-Turn

"Phay Phay, can you come into the cockpit with me?" Mimi was pulling on his arm, and he got up and followed her to the front of the plane. They were now in the crowded cockpit with three other passengers, and I succumbed to the pleasure of the moment amid the "oohs" and "aahs" as people scrambled from one side of the plane to the other.

As the gigantic mountains loomed larger than life, peak after incredible peak, I could not take in all the grandeur and was truly grateful that these never-to-be-forgotten moments could be captured on digital cameras.

"This is Captain Abraham speaking. Please take a look out the windows. This is the highlight of our expedition." Breathtaking in its grandeur and majesty, and where some had lost their lives, Mt. Everest stood unparalleled. It was mind-boggling that we were passing right over the peak of the highest mountain in the world. It was exhilarating to realize we were viewing the heights that Hillary and Tensing and other daring mountain climbers had scaled—those which had led over torturous, icy, dangerous, virgin pathways that could easily cause an icy death.

Yet these spectacular views were ours for just a moment as time seemed to stand still, and we watched the individual shapes of each mountaintop we hovered over. Pristine snowcapped mountains spoke loudly of the grandeur of their Creator.

"I cannot believe I was able to get all these pictures." Pe hugged me jubilantly as he slipped into the seat beside me. "Wait till I show the others."

On our journey back, the plane made a U-turn, majestically hovering over the same mountain peaks, staying within the Nepalese border that separated us from the neighboring countries.

Given a second chance to view these mountains, I joined the other passengers, rushing to the cockpit and the windows to capture scenes we would preserve and treasure. Anything we missed the first time was made available to us once more.

As we sat back down in our seats, Pe put his arms around me. "Do you know the thought that crossed my mind as the captain turned the plane around?"

I shook my head no.

"You know how I tease you and call you 'Mrs.-Should-Have' when you feel you've missed your one and only chance at something? That amazing U-turn[1] drew a beautiful picture for me of God's grace. It made me think of His infinite love for the world He created and the people He fashioned in His own image."

Pe gently turned me to face him. "God is constantly giving. He's the provider of infinite second chances. There are no failures in His forgiving heart. He is so gracious and compassionate that He will never turn anyone away from His love, and if anyone wants to be His own, once His, He never lets go."[2]

With his eyelids closed ever so slightly, Pe whispered in my ear, "When I think of His love, it is love unending. Love indescribable! A love that gave all! His arms were even stretched out on the cross, welcoming everyone with an everlasting love, as He gave Himself to the people He longed to embrace."

My hand tucked under his, I nestled my head on his shoulder, and I felt safe with this amazing man who was so secure in his Father's love.

Suddenly, I bolted upright in my seat. A U-turn! A second chance!

Startled, Pe turned and stared at me.

I could barely control the excitement in my voice. "I know now why I have been brought to Nepal! This place has forced me to relive my childhood memories. I have been carrying this burden for so long, knowing I need to write my story. I have always put it on the back burner with the excuse that I didn't have time. But it has been eating away at me, and when I get back to Chattanooga, I will begin to write.

Pe smiled and promptly dozed off again.

Soon we touched down, and no one could stop talking about what a thrill our journey had been. The road back to the Kathmandu hotel was bumpy. With my head laid back comfortably on the headrest and my fingers entwined with Pe's, I let my thoughts float back to my young Burma days. But this time, I did so with nostalgia and thanks to the God of second chances, who had set me free.

Chapter 3

Snapshots of My Childhood

If I find in myself a desire which no experience
in this world can satisfy,
the most probable explanation
is that I was made for another world.
–C. S. Lewis[1]

Burma, 1940s

My father, enlisted by the British King, George VI, was still in the Royal Navy when my sister Esme and I were born in war-torn Burma. At a time when both the English and the Japanese were fighting on Burmese soil, Rangoon, our city, had become a hot spot in World War II. In one of my grandfather's gripping stories about the old Burma days, he mused, "Japanese soldiers did not spare anyone they thought looked British. Many of the Anglo Indian and Eurasian families had to escape for cover to the neighboring villages. Many trekked to India to escape from their beloved Burma."

My grandfather seemed old in my young tween years. Still, his mind was remarkable as he solved mathematical equations, including algebra and trigonometry, in his head without writing them on paper.

Exam time found my cousin and me quizzing his brain so we would get top grades. "Pho Pho, can you help us, please? We have no idea how to calculate this."

I never tired of hearing him tell stories of his young life. He always spoke with a clipped British accent. "My marriage to your grandmother was arranged while I was away at Cambridge University. As soon as I received my engineering degree, I came back from England to claim my bride. Did you know she had been betrothed to me since she was seven years old?"

He was an elegant man, well-versed in every subject, and had become a political figure before I was born. My grandmother reveled in being the wife of a prominent national figure. "Your grandfather was the Lord Mayor of Rangoon, a member of Parliament, and was loved by the people and respected by the officials of Burma and the British Consulate."

I had heard it a hundred times, but my grandmother would continue, "Did you know that your grandfather received an audience with King George Frederick Ernest Albert, King of the United Kingdom and the British dominions and Emperor of India from 1910 to 1936?"

He was landed gentry, wealthy by virtue of his birth, the eldest son of U Ohn who had built an empire on teak and was one of the richest men of his time. A major road had been named after him, presumably remaining to this day, unless the fickle military government has changed its name because of some fortune teller or palm reader.

Born in a Trench

I can picture my grandfather leaning forward in his armchair, chin in hand, his voice trailing off at times as he recounted the details of my birth. But more often than not, he would punctuate his sentences almost as if he were right there.

"It was March 29, 1944," he said, looking at me intently as though he were being interviewed by a talk show host. "As bombs thundered overhead and the piercing sounds of machine guns split the night air, your mother remained hidden in a deep trench."

He stopped and scratched his head. "Working quietly in the light of your Uncle Robert's flashlight, the midwife expertly and quietly delivered you from your mother's womb. With no access to a hospital, your mother and you seemed to have flourished well..." His voice trailed off, his eyes seemed far away, and he nodded off to sleep. I was always amazed at how I had been allowed a safe entrance into the world with danger all around.

Stories about my birth always thrilled me. My father often shared his personal experience, which I thought was exciting: "I had rowed for several nights in a flat-bottomed boat called a sampan. It was very stressful trying to hide from the Japanese soldiers. They would have taken me at gunpoint or shot me in the head." He looked at me. "I was forced to lay low in the swamps during the day. It was such a dangerous and lonely journey, traveling through the enemy camp, but I wanted to be with you and Mummy and Esme, even if just for a few days."

Daddy's stay was short, and he made the return journey the same way he came, but we remained in Maubin and did not return to our country home in Rangoon until Britain and its allied troops drove the Japanese soldiers out of Burma.

How could I have known then, living in Rangoon and pampered with all the luxuries given to me as a privileged child, that riches would never fill the emptiness of my heart and quiet the gnawing feeling that there could be something more?

Even at that young age, I felt such an emptiness in my soul. So I set out on a search for something that would still the restless, relentless longing I did not understand.

Chapter 4

Life in Rangoon at the Height of its Glory Days

For the temple bells are callin', an' it's there that I would be
By the old Moulmein Pagoda, looking lazy at the sea;
On the road to Mandalay, Where the flyin-fishes play,
An' the dawn comes up like thunder outer china 'crost the Bay
—Rudyard Kipling[1]

Rangoon, 1950s

Burma, the Land of the Pagodas, forever immortalized by the British poet Rudyard Kipling's poem "Mandalay," won its independence from the British monarchy on January 4, 1948, one year and one day after my younger sister Gail Georgiana was born.

Many British immigrants, who had learned to love this rich and unspoiled country and made lifelong friends with the gentle Burmese people, remained on Burmese soil and made Rangoon their permanent home.

Mrs. Emma Smith-Jones, one of the charming ladies from the British Embassy, had invited my mother and me to her home one gorgeous summer day in 1950 for the first of many treasured visits. Above her pergola, thick, vibrant leaves and hanging wisteria grew together with climbing cabbage roses, giving off a heavenly scent.

I loved listening to her stories, which she wove with such joy and humor. She lived through the war and then embraced Rangoon as it quickly became a growing cosmopolitan English-speaking, friendly city rich in history and culture.

"The grandeur of the city was at its height when we bought this home." She'd pause with a twinkle in her eye and a deep chuckle in her throat. "Your parents, their friends, and I partied at all the foreign embassies, joined the exclusive golf and tennis clubs, and frequented the up-and-coming major department stores, where money could provide all the luxuries we wanted." She continually regaled me with antics of their younger days, and we regularly ended up in stitches.

Sir John Geoffrey Smith-Jones, her more serious husband, often joined the end of our conversation. "I am so thankful that the English and American schools in Rangoon offer education from kindergarten through high school and that all the textbooks and reference books for history, geography, algebra, geometry, trigonometry, physics, and chemistry are all in English." He picked up his son's picture and smiled. "English literature and language together with Burmese literature were compulsory subjects, and Geoffrey Jr. excelled."

Miss Emma would chuckle. "My Geoffrey still talks about his school days here. He and Catherine met and fell in love in their junior year and couldn't wait to get married. I am so glad that we decided to live in Rangoon. Otherwise, they would never have met."

"I am glad too, Miss Emma, that you did not go back to London. I am so happy that you and Mummy are such good friends."

With an Everlasting Love

There was a warmth in that home that never failed to grip my heart. The walls were adorned with beautiful pictures, but what caught my eye every time were the Scripture verses inscribed on so many of them. One especially filled me with a hunger for something that seemed so familiar yet so elusive: "I have loved you with an everlasting love, therefore with loving kindness have I drawn you. –Jeremiah 31:3." The beautiful calligraphy had been done by a famous artist.

I was lost in thought when I heard a gentle rustle. Miss Emma had pulled out a clipping of a gossip column she had kept from a three-year-old newspaper. It was captioned "Who's Who."

She patted the seat next to her on the sofa, tucked my hand under her arm, and read, "The elite lived, worked, socialized, and pursued an education on par with the best schools and universities in England. The landed gentry of the elite Burmese crowd lived in several-storied multi-bedroom, mullioned-windowed homes with massive, sprawling grounds, manicured lawns, tennis courts, and swimming pools. The foreign ambassadors' children grew up, played tennis and hockey, swam, had parties, and attended private English or American schools with the Burmese youth of the favored group."

She smiled as she folded the clipping and put it away.

This was the Burma I had known. This was the country that had afforded me the best education. This was the culture that shaped me and gave me lifelong friends.

As we said goodbye to Sir John Geoffrey and Miss Emma and drove away down their long and winding driveway, my mind would return to that familiar Jeremiah 31:3 verse on her living room wall. I looked at the words every single time we were in their warm and welcoming home. Something about that picture seemed to squeeze my heart.

Who was the person who said, "I have loved you with an everlasting love"? And what did he mean when he said he had drawn with loving kindness whomever he was speaking to? Would I find a love like that? One which would last forever? Was there really such a love that could draw somebody?

Chapter 5

Across the Oceans

The perpetual cadence of the vast sea,
Stirs a restless desire that engulfs me.
Like an infinite force I dare not impede,
Briefly rushing in—only then to recede.
Beckoning me to leave life's safe shore,
Into deep waters of mystery and lore.
–Belinda Stotler[1]

Early 1950s, Rangoon

Once the war was over, Daddy left the Royal Navy and joined the local branch of the P&O Shipping Lines, recognized as the world's oldest cruise line, which was headquartered in London, England. By that time, my younger sister, Gail Georgianna, was four years old, and I was almost seven.

I remember our family often traveling on cruise ships throughout my childhood and teenage years on all of Daddy's "home leaves" to England. Every three years, London became our home for four months of the year. I adored London, which was considered home to those who had been among the elite with the company, and it was fun to be with our British cousins and my Scottish uncle.

"In those early days, the cruises across the ocean to Britain were often several weeks long," Mummy recalled later. "We had to travel around the Cape of Good Hope before the Suez Canal was built, and you girls could not wait to get off the ship."

My youngest sister, Maureen Phillipa, was ten years younger than me, and I immediately took her under my wing from the minute she was placed into my arms. In 1955, at barely a year old, she first learned to speak in complete sentences on one of those trips. I can still hear her little, high-pitched voice chanting, "I can see Mummy, I can see Daddy," in a charming British accent.

Most of our high-society friends spoke in English, and our home was no exception. This included all our household help except for our maids and one chauffeur.

Esme, Gail, Maureen, and I were privileged to travel widely with our parents. I have forgotten how many ports of call we stopped at on our home leave cruises—Gibraltar, Malta, and Athens, among others in the West. In the East, we visited Singapore, Penang, Borneo, Kuala Lumpur, Ceylon (now Sri Lanka), many parts of India, and other exotic places. All of them were, to me, real, live educational experiences.

Shipwrecked

When I was nine, I clearly remember what I thought was quite an exciting adventure. We had just set sail on the *Sangola*, one of our cruise ships. Then, lying on the top bunk in our state cabin, I heard a *boom*, repeated by a louder *boom*! Then, a thunderous *crack*! I placed my hands on my ears to deaden the sound of men yelling, "Get out! Get out!" and the heavy footsteps hurrying past our cabin door.

A crackling sound came over a loudspeaker. Then came the captain's voice. "*Sangola* has run into a sand bank close to the Indian shore, and it is breaking in half. Prepare to get off the ship immediately by lining up in your designated areas. We will take you in lifeboats to the shore."

Separated in the pandemonium, Mummy, who had barely been able to rescue her two Siamese kittens, had already been placed in a boat heading toward shore. Daddy was on another small vessel with Esme and Gail, and I was carried aloft on the shoulders of a crew member.

Waves pummeled the lifeboat I was in as it struck out for shore. I was wet and shaking with fright as I was finally brought to land and reunited with my family, who had been frantically searching for me. "Where were you, Tita?" Daddy caught me up in his arms. "I looked all over for you."

"I was so scared, but I knew you would find me."

"We were so worried." Mummy had brought a change of clothes and was drying me with a towel. "I thought you were with Esme and Gail, and Daddy thought you were with me."

Happy to be found, I ran off to look for Esme and Gail to tell them about my great adventure.

A Taste of India

At one point, my studies were interrupted because my father's company transferred him to India for two years. We were taken to an Indian businessman's home in transit to Calcutta, where, strangely enough, I vividly remember the exotic dinner we were served. Mr. Raju explained, "This is called *puri*; it is a fluffy Indian bread. You eat it with this hot vegetable curry. It is very good, but it might burn your tongue and the roof of your mouth."

Seeing my look of concern, he said. "Don't worry. You can cool it down with this mango *lassi* drink." Hurrying into the kitchen, he came back with a tray of goodies. "Taste this Indian sweet. It is made of cream and thinly sliced almonds. It will melt in your mouth and make you want to eat more!"

We lived in Calcutta and then briefly in Bombay (now Mumbai). It was a challenging time as I had to study Hindi and Bengali at the International School we attended. We learned Hindu and Muslim prayers in both languages at the school in Calcutta. It was disconcerting for me because I was also praying my Buddhist prayers before I went to bed. *How many gods are there?* I wondered. *Do they all listen at the same time?*

I searched for something that seemed to become more elusive with the passing of time. I felt an unrest I could not put my finger on.

Chapter 6

Naan, Puri, Lentils, Lamb Curry, and Brass Gongs

Memory is the diary that we all carry about with us.
−Oscar Wilde[1]

February 7, 2014, Kathmandu Hotel

I felt a slight jolt as my mind was brought back to the present. The car bringing us back from the airport had come to a sudden standstill at a busy crossroad as we drove into the city of Kathmandu. Here I was, back in an Indian culture. Half-forgotten images were coming at me from everywhere. *Sensory overload,* I thought to myself. *Process it all later. It's too much now. Be in the moment. Be mindful of what's going on in the present.*

A herd of cows was crossing the street ever so slowly. I smiled. This had been a familiar scene when I lived in India. I was glad I had been exposed to different lands and cultures as a young child and had learned to adapt to the places we traveled to. The big cow following up the rear let out a big "Moo" and ambled after the others, making way for us to get through.

I rolled down the window and stuck my head out of the car. The smell of barbequed kebabs and skewered tandoori chicken from a nearby road restaurant wafted toward us, making me hungry.

The open-air shops on the side of the road held knickknacks of every shape and color.

"Come, madame. Come, sir. Come in and see what we have for you!" shopkeepers called out to passersby, hawking their wares. The sights, the smells, the sounds, and the clamor were all part of the charm of a place unchanged by modern sophistication.

A delightful Indian dinner awaited us on our return to the hotel. "Look, Darling, the naan and *puri* breads are just like the ones your cook used to make." Pe piled a couple of them on his plate and went over to the lavish buffet. "And look at that lentil dish!"

The chef came out of the kitchen to greet us. He was holding a huge casserole dish with both hands. "I cooked this *biriyani* dish especially for you to enjoy!" He lifted the lid, and the aroma of cumin, coriander seeds, cinnamon bark, and bay leaves was enticing; the tandoori-baked chicken in the spiced rice made our mouths water.

"There is also chicken, shrimp, lamb, and potato curries. Over here is tandoori chicken and skewed kebabs. You might also like to try the *moilee*. It is a mild fish curry with coconut sauce." He beamed with pride, "Let me bring out more of the *paratha* bread."

We filled up our plates with a sampling of everything on the buffet table—including the mint sauce, the sweet chutney, and the mild mango pickle—and sat down at the long dinner table with the snowy white tablecloth.

It all reminded me so much of the life I once left behind.

Waking up to Brass Gongs and Jasmine on the Breeze
February 10, 2014, Kathmandu Hotel

I opened my eyes and saw the golden sunlight streaming in through the gossamer-covered casement window. Kathmandu, day six of our conference stay in Nepal. Beside me was my gently breathing husband. At the foot of the bed, my daughter lay curled up on a pullout bed. The familiar sounds of softly beating mallets upon brass gongs came lightly to my ears. The smell of jasmine abloom outside the open windows came slowly wafting in as I took deep breaths in a familiar moment from yesteryear. *Where would my thoughts lead me?* I wondered as the sweet perfume of jasmine permeated the room.

Gardens! My mind raced back to our own lush gardens back home in Rangoon, where my mother found the beauty that had been missing from her life. She did not care for the jewelry and the clothing that women in her sphere sought after. Instead, fresh cut flowers of every shape and hue in beautiful cut crystal vases spread throughout the spacious rooms of our country home brought her joy and comfort.

My young and impressionable heart soaked up the quiet strength and beauty of her soul. Her love of nurturing and watching her plants grow and her delight in their fragrance, colors, and diverse shapes and sizes birthed in me the desire to embrace and cultivate what was lost or hidden in the very depth of my being.

Chapter 7

Gardens, Bridges, and Swans
on a Placid Lake

Memory is a way of holding on to the things you love,
the things you are, the things you never want to lose.
–Kevin Arnold[1]

Late 1950s – Garden Home, Golden Valley, Rangoon, Burma

"Suri, the gardenia plants are starting to bloom," my mother said. "Let's cut some stems so the flowers can open up and fill the parlor with their lovely scent."

"Yes, Memsahib Eve, I will get some shears." Suri promptly returned with an empty basket and two clippers. Then she and I followed my mother down the garden path.

Along the front of the house, partly skirting the huge oval-shaped, manicured lawn, was a pond edged by my mother's phlox in hues of brilliant colors. When looking at it, in my mind's eye, I saw a hazy picture of majestic white swans on the placid lake, reminding me of my beloved ballet class.

I felt like a swan as I danced in Madame Francoise's class. She had been my teacher for over eleven years and had instilled grace, beauty, and flow in both my movements and thoughts. Strangely, she saw something in my six-year-old self I had not yet recognized. "Child, you never relax! You must learn to relax. Breathe in slowly and release. Enjoy the moment and dance with a free and flowing heart."

With every dance movement I learned, I replayed her wise advice. Yet back in our home and away from her studio, where I danced to the beautiful strains of *Swan Lake*, I was still a tight little ball of unnamed worry and constant stress. I kept my excellent grades and was charming and kind to everyone I met, but always lurking in the background was a strange uneasiness. Did it have anything to do with the tug-of-war going on in my heart?

Our spacious home held many memories for me. There, Aunt Phyllis combed my hair and swept it into a sleek chignon, sharing, "The land your grandfather inherited is enormous. He gave away several acres to a Buddhist monastery, but there is still enough land for the maids, butler, cook, and their families—including our gardeners and chauffeurs. And acres beyond that for all his descendants to build houses and gardens."

All the household help occupied the far side of the property. The grounds also contained a driveway winding nearly three miles from the gate to the main residence, several hedged gardens, multiple tennis courts, and a gigantic stone-walled swimming pool.

In the height of its glorious days, when it had been meticulously maintained, it must have been a place of enchantment—a hideaway in the center of the city. And though much of it now was in disrepair, for us as children, it was a mecca of fun—offering places to hide, trees to climb, and plentiful space to ride our bikes.

The Shadow of Things to Come

When I was about seven or eight years old, I often played hide and seek with my sisters and cousins, and the broken-walled swimming pool was one of my favorite hideaway places. My cousin Jenny and I had many weekend sleepovers. We would raid the larder, putting our newly acquired picnic food in tiny little pots and pans and then sitting on the grass under a tree to enjoy our "cooking" straight from the pots.

Jenny and I were inseparable. We did our homework together and listened to her dad teach us the basics of mathematical equations. We were the same age and attended the same school where we were in the same grades from kindergarten to high school. Memories of those carefree days stayed with both of us through the upcoming years of turmoil.

Years later, Jenny and I would meet after having been forcibly separated for nearly thirty years, torn apart by a powerful military regime. After she married, her husband was forced to leave Burma, escaping through the jungle and, eventually, making his way to Washington, DC. Although Jenny secretly stayed in touch with him, they did not see each other for seven years— until Jenny also escaped through the Burmese jungle with her two small daughters. Their family finally reconnected, as her husband met his younger daughter for the first time.

How could we have known, as children without a care in the world, that our lives would be so brutally shattered?

Chapter 8

Growing Up in Luxury

*Memories play a very confusing role, they make us laugh
when we remember the times we cried but make us cry
when we remember the times we laughed!*
–Unknown[1]

Every day, our home was full of excitement. The minute Esme, Gail, Maureen, and I arrived home from school, we would climb the mango trees and then run to the cook to have him slice our juicy findings.

In our young adult years, the conveniently long driveway, bordered on both sides by trees, was the perfect place to secretly learn to drive our friends' cars, as we were only allowed to ride in daddy's chauffeur-driven vehicles.

The two gardeners, our *marlies*, kept our lawns green and manicured and, under my mother's tutelage, tended gardens profuse with flowers of all varieties and shades.

Flame of the forest trees, ablaze in bright red, along with other flowering trees bursting with magnolia blossoms, delicate frangipani flowers, and bougainvillea blooms, lined the long driveway, creating a cheerful and elegant welcome to the portico of our house.

Fruit trees clustered here and there sported luscious mangoes, specialty marian plums, golden and red bananas, jackfruit, guavas, and other exotic delicacies. Coconut trees were plentiful, and we would have our *marlies,* who tucked up their sarong-like *loungyis* to their waist, shimmy up the slender swaying palms and bring down the coconuts so we could savor the sweet, translucent liquid.

Mummy chose the flowers she wanted to have planted and gave instructions daily for the flowers to be cut. The floral arrangements that adorned the formal solid mahogany dining table that seated sixteen people were my special delight. Sitting on the snowy white damask tablecloths in the presence of the masterfully crafted yet understated table settings that included the sparkling crystal glasses, heirloom silverware, bone china dinnerware settings, and snowy white napkins which were painstakingly shaped into stunning art, the carefully crafted floral centerpiece picked for the day was always an explosion of joyful color.

Creamy Silk Shirts, Butlers, and Sticky Fingers

My father wore creamy silk shirts with elegant gold cufflinks, expensive club ties, and custom-made suits. One evening at dinner, my sister Gail surreptitiously wiped her sticky fingers under the table on what she thought was the edge of the white tablecloth, only to find to her chagrin, that she had smeared fingerprints on Daddy's white silk trousers while he was turning toward the butler who had brought him his evening newspaper. After that incident, my sister either moved herself or was moved farther down from the head of the table—beyond the reach of my father's exquisite clothing.

Mani was my father's butler. He was a kind, loyal, and faithful man who brought our letters on a silver platter and took excellent care of my father. His flawless skin was the color of dark mahogany, and his ordinarily stern face showed gleaming white teeth when he smiled.

"Sahib, I have pressed the trousers for tonight. Would you like me to steam your silk shirt?" Turning around to Mummy, "Memsahib, would you like me to place the mail on your writing desk or on the sideboard?" Faithful Mani made sure all the household needs were met, and we all loved him as part of our family.

Tall and elegant, Mani was of the Hindu faith, a strict vegetarian, very religious, serious and proper, and always meticulously dressed in a white butler's uniform lined with gold buttons. I think I was his favorite protégé. "Miss Nita," he would say, "Big Missy has eaten up all the cake I left for you and the small missies. I will have the cook bake another one."

Sisters

We had three Burmese live-in maids who looked after all our needs, including making our beds, taking care of our clothes, and serving us at mealtimes. "Is there anything you want me to do for you?" they would ask, standing at attention as soon as we got out of bed.

I was a rather independent little girl, but Esme had her maid at her beck and call. "I need my slippers. Where are they?" "Have you ironed my silk *htamein* and *aingyi*?"

A cleaning crew regularly came and washed the windows and polished our already-shining hardwood floors, balconies, and rails. We had fun sliding across the mirror-like floors in our school socks, pretending we were on a skating rink.

My sister Gail Georgianna was three years younger than me. She was the daredevil offspring of George and Eve. I think she was named after Daddy, who hoped his third child would be a boy. She would sit astride the smooth banister, facing backward, and slide down two floors. And she loved to make me sit on a slippery bamboo mat with her, giggling as we bumped all the way down the steps while I hung on the edge, petrified I would break my tailbone. Gail would hoot, "Wasn't that fun?" "Let's do it again!" And although she broke her elbow twice, she still delighted in climbing and jumping off beds and tall cupboards, constantly pushing herself to the limit.

Our laundry man also lived on the property. He would pick up our clothes every day to hand wash and dry them. Always dressed in white, Raju wore a loose Indian cotton shirt and flowing muslin trousers tucked between his legs to make his walking smoother and unhampered. His shaved head and thin ponytail growing out from the back of his head was, I believe, a Hindu tradition. His beaming smile showed crooked yellow teeth, and he always seemed happy. "Good morning, missy," he would say, "I washed all your school uniforms early this morning. They are drying on the wash line. I will soon give them to your maids."

Two chauffeurs were hired to drive us to school and other activities. Ko Mya Maung, a gentle and reserved Burman, was the head driver. He always chauffeured us—the four daughters—and religiously obeyed Daddy's strict orders, ensuring we would arrive and leave on time.

Ko Mya Maung escorted us to the few parties we were permitted to attend, and by Daddy's express wishes, he waited for us in the driveway of the party house. Much to our eternal embarrassment, if we did not come to the designated place where the car was at precisely 8 p.m., he would toot the horn or come in and get us himself.

Schockard was the chauffeur who usually drove Daddy around. A small and unusual man, he was Indian by birth, had protruding yellow eyes and a shock of jet-black hair that strangely contrasted his nutmeg skin and the shiny gold buttons on his white uniform. He was such fun to be around and would often bring the house down without even trying.

He was always getting into trouble with my dad. "I didn't do it, Sahib. I don't know who did that, but I didn't do it." He had a high-pitched voice and was always denying blame for everything that he either had not listened to or had been careless about. He was, however, an obliging man who tripped over himself trying to please everybody.

Celebrating Christmas in a Buddhist Home

Although ours was a Buddhist-Hindu home, Christmas, with all its external trimmings, played a big part in my childhood. For our family, Christmas Eve was a time when merchants, contractors, and all who depended on their contracts with the shipping firm brought all kinds of presents. Indian merchants would roll up in their luxury cars, bow low, and say, "Thank you, Sahib, we are very grateful to you."

Our house became full of pastries, European chocolates, Belgian waffles, Indian delicacies, and exotic fruit. My favorites were the Christmas cakes baked in the British tradition with almond icing decorating a moist fruit cake and steamed fruit-laden English puddings covered with brandy, lit with a match and flaming, paired with butter sauce.

On Christmas morning, we would open our stockings, presumably from Santa Clause. Every year Esme would ask me, "What did you get?" And when I told her, she would say, "Why, that is exactly what I wanted." Esme was gentle-natured but persuasive. The first-born child, she usually got her way. "I want to have that one. Will you exchange it with me for one of my presents?"

I always gave in. "I don't mind. You can choose anything you want."

Santa's stocking time was followed by a steaming breakfast of every imaginable treat—except beef, which was not eaten because the cow was considered sacred. After lunch, Mummy sorted Christmas presents from under a gigantic Christmas tree, and Daddy distributed the beautifully wrapped gifts of varying shapes and sizes.

The Christmas dinner goose fiasco with Schockard occurred when I was about twelve years old and remains high on my list of memories. The entire family and guests were seated at the family table. The first and second courses were being cleared off the table when Schockard, who had been enlisted to help Mani and the cook, appeared prematurely with a huge oval platter laden with three succulent geese.

Balancing the heavy platter, which Mani usually carried with a flourish, was a Herculean task for tiny Schockard, who had taken on the responsibility unasked. And the polished floor was slippery. As he passed Mani, standing at attention behind Daddy's chair, he yelled, "The goose is coming!" And he unceremoniously slipped and fell on his back, still bravely balancing aloft the silver platter holding the geese.

Without blinking an eyelid, Mani retrieved the platter from Schockard's shaking hands and, in his stoic fashion, set it on the polished mahogany sideboard and proceeded to slice the goose for all of us, now in hysterics—except for Daddy, who didn't think it was funny.

Our cook was unforgettable. Trained as a Cordon Bleu chef at the British embassy before he was conscripted to work for my father, he regularly provided us with five-course meals fit for a royal household.

We were not allowed to go to the kitchen, which was in the other wing of the house, but I would try to write down notes for him on different recipes whenever I could. "Raj, how did you make your wonderful pumpkin soup? I would love to learn how to make it."

"Missy, I show you next time."

From childhood, I learned to use the proper place settings during our very formal meals. Fish or steak knife? Salad fork, dinner fork, dessert fork. Dinner spoon, dessert spoon, teaspoon. How each is to be placed and how and when each is to be used.

Such was the luxury that surrounded us, the service we were accustomed to, and the endless privileges of the elite class that we took for granted. I did not know life as it existed beyond my sheltered boundaries, but soon, I would.

I Am Not Enough

Our meals were in the English tradition: breakfast at 7 a.m., lunch at noon, teatime at 4 p.m., and dinner at 7 p.m. This happened like clockwork, and we had to come into the formal dining room properly attired. My father, brought up in England by an overly strict aunt, kept a very orderly life and strict household. "The tablecloth is not straight, Mani. Please make sure that it hangs evenly from both sides."

We were taught to be punctual, do everything in a neat and orderly fashion, be polite, be seen and not heard, study hard, and excel. But our best efforts to be correct never seemed to be enough for Daddy. Now I know this was not the case, but at that age, I felt that if I wanted to be accepted, I needed to be perfect. I tried hard to please and became anxious if I thought I had failed.

I learned to be a good girl, to be quiet and reserved. I became the daughter who packed Daddy's golf bag, the sister who took care of her two younger siblings, and the person who always tried to keep peace in the household.

According to the Buddhist belief, my good deeds would earn me rewards in my next existence. Was that true? Who would be the one to make sure I was given all the merits that I earned in this life? Was there a super being in charge of tallying up my good deeds and striking it off against my bad deeds? Could I do enough?

We wanted for nothing, yet each of us, privileged as we were, had our own private demons to deal with. For me, unnamed but still lurking in the background was emptiness and a vague feeling there was something more—even while I was living a full life of studies, sports, competition, burying myself in the books I loved, and taking joy in my art and ballet.

"Is there really something more?" I kept asking myself repeatedly. But the answer seemed elusive.

Chapter 9

A Pivotal Time in the Life of Our Family

Your life is fleeting, here one moment and gone the next.
The choices we make define us, good and bad.
The love we show strengthens us, furious or left wanting.
The person we choose will change us, for better or worse.
For this life is a passing vapor in the wind,
and the choices we make along the journey will alter the course
–Justin Young.[1]

My father was paid in British pound sterling, a favored exchange money for the Burmese government treasury. At a time when luxury goods were hard to come by, we would have the finest of anything we wanted because of my father's status in the British India Steam Navigation Company, where he had worked for decades. Imports from the ocean liners were regularly brought to our home for us to enjoy.

As a member of high society, my father was given membership at exclusive clubs, met dignitaries, threw lavish parties, and was a well-known figure in the economic world. Outwardly, he was the life and soul of the party, but

I learned later in life that inwardly, he was a lost and lonely child always trying to please, who never felt quite worthy enough.

My parents' social calendars were full, leaving very little time for each other or their four daughters. "George, we would love for you and Evelyn to join us at our annual Australian Ball. We are expecting a large crowd, and I believe you will enjoy the guests who have been invited." "Hello, old chap, we are planning a dinner party in the formal dining hall of the British Embassy, and you and Eve will be getting an invitation soon." "Mr. George Ohn, I am the new Laotian ambassador. My wife and I would like to meet you and your family." "This is Admiral Douglas Scott. We would love the honor of having you and your wife dine with us on our ship for our tenth-anniversary celebration. We will be entering port tomorrow and will send a tender for you." "Hi George, my wife and I would like to have you and Eve over to the US embassy for cocktails and snacks."

Daddy was already a covenanted officer for the P&O Lines because of his seniority, and by the time my youngest sister, Maureen Phillipa—whom we now lovingly called Chicky—was born, he was next in line to become the executive director of the Burma branch.

"Girls, the Senior Director of McKinnon McKenzie will be retiring, and we need to make plans to move to the company's luxury apartments so we can be closer to Daddy's work. We will still have our garden home, and you can come back for weekends."

Daddy took on the helm of the executive administration; this was a pivotal turn in our family's life. We moved from our family home to a spacious apartment in the city close to the Rangoon harbor, where we spent our tween and teen years.

We hardly saw our parents because they had to attend innumerable dinners and parties on and off the ships, take dignitaries and distinguished guests on golfing and shopping expeditions, and mix with the elite at ballroom dances at exclusive clubs where Daddy belonged. We got used to hearing things like, "Come on, Eve, we need to get ready to go to the US Ambassador's house. Schockard will have the car ready in twenty minutes. Mani, can you press my cummerbund and cream silk shirt and put out my gold cufflinks?"

Everything To Be Thankful For

Mani, always Daddy's butler, took on a new role when our parents were away from the house. "Missy," he would tell me, "Your mum has asked me to make sure you have your dinners on time and that you are taken and brought back from school." He hesitated, "Big Missy does not want to listen to me. Will you help me with her?"

"Of course, Mani, I will."

Esme did not like anybody telling her what to do, but she liked my "suggestions." We all worked well together.

Mani was reserved and quiet, but he was full of wisdom. I liked talking to him. "Mani, you have been looking after Daddy for a long, long time, and now you take care of all of us too. Are you happy here?"

"Missy, I have everything to be thankful for. My life before I came here was not easy. I was brought into your home to take care of your father, but you have all treated me like family, and my heart is full. Your father treats me well even though he doesn't show it. He has a good heart and is very generous."

Works of Art

Life in the city was hectic; Mummy was kept busy. But she always found time to make sure we were well cared for and tried to spend as much time as possible on our school and home life.

She no longer had her beloved gardens to tend but continued her beautiful needlepoint. With her deft hands, she allowed her imagination to have full reign as she created works of art that I will always treasure. A beautiful tapestry that now hangs in my living room displays bursts of color in picturesque outdoor scenes.

Oil paintings, watercolors, stick figures, silhouettes in black and white, and charcoal and pencil drawings—all captured on linen, canvas, vellum, or even scrap paper—pictured the innermost feelings of a creative soul.

Then there was the embroidery, cross stitch, smocking, intricate beading, and pretty ruffles she handstitched onto the beautiful dresses she cut out and sewed for her four daughters.

This treasure of handiwork brought joy and color into her life where dreams had been crushed and her tender heart, once filled with hope, was slowly being trampled. She loved her husband, and she knew he loved her. But despite their love and his provision for her every need, they were worlds apart.

While Daddy lived the life of a successful businessman and continued the search for fame and pleasure as the only son of wealthy, landed gentry, I sensed that the pleasure of being the wife of a rich, successful man did not hold enchantment for Mummy in the continually moving social circles foreign to her nature. The two moved further and further apart until the only thing that held them together was their four daughters.

This sadness, I felt, had intensified her artistic talent and brought some form of fulfillment for her in a life where spring had died in her marriage. What gave her the strength?

Sitting at my mother's side were my happiest moments. As I watched her deft fingers move, I learned about her patience, peace, and sense of accomplishment, and I gained a true appreciation for her quietness of soul and mind. We had a quiet companionship where we didn't have to speak, and I bonded with her as I learned from her.

"Nita," she would say, "you are the only one who truly loves what I love. I love your generous and serving heart. You are a very special person, and you will always be a special daughter to me."

All this craftsmanship, the love for art and beautiful gardens, romantic poetry, and music were passed down to me, her second daughter.

But I inherited much more than that. My mother's strength of character and quiet trust in what I learned was her God, along with her loyalty and acceptance in every situation God brought into her life, became a beautiful example I longed to follow.

I would often think of Mrs. Emma's picture. That verse was imprinted in my mind and on my heart. *I have loved you with an everlasting love, therefore with loving kindness I have drawn you.* I wanted to be loved and drawn to someone who would lavish on me this everlasting love, who would draw me with loving kindness. Was there such a someone somewhere?

Chapter 10

A Search for Something More

I see myself as a man who is searching for meaning in life.
This is rather different from being a staunch believer in something.
A believer is someone who senses
a consciousness or a direction and believes in it.
The one who searches for meaning has not found the direction yet.
–Aharon Appelfeld[1]

My mother was the second daughter of Ma Kyai and Donald Urquhart. A pure Burmese lady who would only speak in her Burmese language, Ma Kyai was betrothed and married at the consent of her parents to the dashing young Scotsman, Donald Urquhart, a barrister-at-law then practicing in Burma. My grandmother was tall, slender, stately, and very serious, and Donald fell madly in love with her. He ardently sought her hand in marriage and won her as a reluctant bride.

But Where's the Bride?

Right from the start, my maternal grandmother and grandfather's marriage was a stormy one. The unsuspecting bride was told by her mother to sew a mosquito netting such as is used in countries where mosquitoes are prevalent. These gossamer white curtains around the bed are very effective in providing a barricade against bothersome, stinging pests.

"Ma Kyai, here is some gossamer netting. It is for a bride, so I want you to make it with a lot of frills. You can use my sewing machine. We can use the silver ribbons to make a pretty sash on each side of the opening, and you can sew sequins along the side."

My grandmother dutifully completed the ornate bridal mosquito net and brought it to her mother. Anger set in on the wedding day when she found out she was the bride.

Marriages were arranged, and daughters had no say in the matter. As I was growing up, I believed that my grandmother was very upset over this—that her trademark seriousness was due to this deception. I associated her refusal to speak in English to her husband, whom I did not have the privilege to meet, with the thought that she felt she should have been asked for her hand in marriage. It was a good thing he spoke Burmese.

"Tell me about your wedding, May May Gyi," I asked. "Did you really not know you were getting married until the day before?"

"Yes, Ni Ni. I was so angry with my parents."

"Are you angry with Granddaddy Urquhart too? Is that why you never spoke to him in English?" She did not answer, but she gave me a little smile.

Footprints of My Mother

To this strangely mismatched couple, my mother was born ten years after the birth of their first daughter, Mary, whom I thought had the sweetest smile. A beautiful Eurasian girl, my mother, Evelyn Grace Urquhart, was a quiet, gentle Christian who eventually taught English at a girls' high school.

Her sister, Mary, also an English teacher, would tell me, "Your mother has all the graces of a well-brought-up English lady. She has this unbelievable strength which has allowed her to bravely face all the hard things she has had to go through." She looked at me as she smiled. "She wore fashionable clothes that she learned to make herself, and each original piece looked very becoming for her slender figure and delicate, chiseled features. As she grew up under my care, I was very proud of her. You remind me of her."

My mother and father's marriage to each other was not arranged. I would ply my father with questions. "Daddy, did you choose whom you wanted to marry?"

His answer made me happy. "Of course I did. It was World War II, and I had just joined the British Royal Navy, where I was conscripted by King George into the Division of the Burma Navy. Mummy was educated, talented, and beautiful. She caught my eye, and I fell head over heels in love with her."

His face lit up. "She will tell you how hard I tried to win her. She was teaching at a girls' convent, and I would climb up on the wall of the school just for a glimpse of her. Mummy did not reciprocate my feelings at first and kept me at arm's length until she finally agreed to become my bride."

Stories of how my Daddy wooed this young teacher who was standing on the threshold of the dreams she envisioned—well-rounded in sporting activities, proficient in sewing, embroidery, and needlepoint, and an amazing artist and painter, steeped in literature and language, who fully used her incredible mind—wove an indelible impression on my seeking heart.

At the top of my "Mommy Memories" list is when she was left sitting spread-eagled on the road, having fallen off from the back seat of my dad's motorcycle. "Did Daddy not realize you had fallen off?"

"I don't think so. I got up, brushed off the back of my skort, and just walked away."

You Don't Belong

My parents, married on December 20, 1941, at the Rangoon town hall, made a handsome couple. Mummy left her teaching career and took on the responsibility of running a well-oiled household where the hired help ran to do her slightest bidding.

Daddy's atrociously wealthy parents, however, were not pleased. They somehow never accepted my mother because she was not of their class and had been required to work for a living.

Their life was exemplified by time spent at the country club, where the wives gathered and gossiped and threw their 10 carat diamond earrings into the coffers to bet on a favorite racehorse. Adding to the issue of her social status, my mother was a Christian. For the most part, my grandmother and her friends ignored my mother's presence. When they weren't ignoring her, they looked down on her as an outcast.

Mummy was labeled as someone who was not a fit bride for the aristocratic Ohn family's only son. She was a spirited young woman who composed herself and prioritized her family and the duties of being a wealthy man's wife.

The Peace of God

My mother had known rejection from childhood. I wondered if she had truly healed from the pain caused by her father, who turned his back on his family after having sired two daughters a decade apart in age. When I asked her, she told me, "When my father deserted us, it forced me to grow up in an orphanage with Aunty Mary. She is my only sister and was the one who truly loved me and the one to whom I clung during my childhood years."

She sat me on the sofa. "Early in my teenage years, I found peace when I met my Jesus. The Bible says it is the peace of God that surpasses all understanding. Jesus is the one who loves us so much that He died for us."

Subconsciously, the verse from Mrs. Emma's painting flashed across my mind. *I have loved you with an everlasting love, therefore with loving kindness I have drawn you.*

"Mummy, does this Jesus love you with an everlasting love? And did He draw you with loving kindness, just like Mrs. Emma's painting says?"

"Yes, Nita, He does love me, and He loves you too. I can see He is drawing you to Him; one day, you will receive Him as your Savior, too. This is a Buddhist household, but I have been praying for Daddy and for all four of you."

Ostracized by her in-laws and often by her husband, who himself had never known what it was to love and be loved, I learned that my mother quietly lived her faith as she ran the household and took care of her husband, her children, and all the hired help.

Her garden of flowers, the flowering shrubs blossoming along the edges of a huge oval-shaped manicured lawn in our country home, and the fruit trees opposite the lake across which she had designed a beautiful walking bridge must have brought her untold joy.

Her needlepoint and all the embroidered dresses she made for her four daughters were surely her delight, as was her daily Bible reading, which she never missed until the day she met her Lord face to face.

Because of her life situation, church-going during her marriage was almost non-existent, but Daddy took it upon himself to chauffeur us to her church every Easter and Christmas. After each of these services, my mother was always excited to meet for a Christmas brunch with a lifelong Christian friend who was also married to a domineering husband.

"Come, girls, put on your pretty dresses. We are going to church with Aunty Martha and her children." Those special "Christian" days were spiritual highlights for me in the Buddhist journey that we children walked in.

My mother was an amazing woman who never once wavered from her Christian faith. Even though she was the odd one out, contentment filled her. Perhaps she had gained this inward joy by allowing her heart to seek meaning despite having an estranged mother who was so wrapped up in a religion that could never satisfy. Or perhaps, having been deserted by her father, she learned she wasn't alone in her suffering when she and her sister were raised by strangers in a children's home. Somewhere, she had discovered that there is someone who cares, whose heart was broken for her, and who would become her solace, her Savior.

As I contemplated this, my heart whispered, "Yes, yes!" How else could my mother have endured and not broken down? How else could her eyes be full of merriment, her laughter quick, and her hands eager to reach out to give to others? How else could she have put the needs of all she took care of above her own?

My mother's gentle life planted beginning seeds in my heart, which in turn raised burning questions that would change my life.

Someday the Silver Cord Will Break

I never knew my mother to complain, and she very rarely shared her grief. I will never forget what she said decades later on the day she was told there were no more treatments left for her aggressive lung cancer, and she knew she would soon die: "I will be ninety in two months, and I have had a good life."

From someone who had known sadness and rejection, her resolve built in me a desire to be thankful, no matter what is brought into my life.

My Father's Mark

My father, George Ohn, like his father before him, was never interested in religion until he was well into his twilight years. Even then, he did not truly understand his Buddhist heritage, but he followed religious tradition, mainly because he felt it was the proper thing to do.

At the end of his life, he leaned on my husband's faith, which seemed to bring him a quiet sense of peace. My father would continually ask my husband to pray, taking comfort that he was being prayed for.

Daddy was an only son, spoiled by the wealth of generations and by his doting, yet rather unaffectionate, mother, who would enlist the chauffeur to drive her infant child around the estate till he fell asleep. He was, in fact, a bewildered and lost child who, deep in his heart, had never known peace.

"Tita, Pe is so good with Zaw and Mimi. My father sent me away for studies in England as a very young child of six to live with a very strict British aunt—your grand aunty Mary—until I was sixteen. She became my only mentor, so I never learned to relax and enjoy my boyhood."

He seemed to have learned to suppress emotions that were never allowed to surface as a young man. And as I watched him try to be a good husband and father, I secretly thought he carried his anger and confusion from childhood into his adult life and his marriage.

I believe my father had a kind heart, but what he revealed to those he silently loved was the exact opposite. He was often demanding and inconsiderate, unable to show his compassion. But I saw another side of him when he took us on picnics in the park and for drives in the countryside when he sang heartfelt songs full of meaning. My sisters and I and Mummy would join in, singing one song after another throughout the trip.

At that time, there were no seat belts, and I delighted in standing on the passenger side and looking out from the sunroof. As I surveyed the landscape and passing cars, I imagined I was flying on the back of a huge eagle. The wind rushing against my face felt cool and delightful. "Be careful, Tita. You might fly off, so hold tight." With that, he stepped on the accelerator just a little bit so that my hair would fly backward, and I would feel the exhilaration of freedom.

From him, Gail Georgianna and I learned to be proficient in management, administration, accounting, and budgeting and work well with personnel. My love for spreadsheets and color coding was due to his amazing organizational gifts. He was a great influencer, and my cousin Chris attributed his social graces to his uncle.

It Is Well with My Soul

I can still see Daddy falling asleep decades later in my mind's eye. It's almost as if it were yesterday. He peacefully smiled as I sang Mummy's hymns to him, his statue of Buddha above his head on a shelf. I believe my Daddy finally found the peace he longed so much for.

Hugs and Kisses

Daddy and Mummy did not know how to show affection with hugs and kisses, which were normal in loving families. Instead, they showed affection by comforting and caring for us. Perhaps Daddy did not grow up feeling comfortable with hugs because none were offered to him, but I know that deep in his heart, he yearned for a love that he did not know how to give.

Chapter 11

My Buddhist Heritage

For me, the teen years were all about
searching for a place for myself,
wondering why I seemed so different than everyone else,
wondering especially why no one could look
past the surface and figure out who I really was underneath.
–Robin Wasserman[1]

Then [with a deep longing] you will seek Me
and require Me [as a vital necessity] and [you will] find Me
when you search for Me with all your heart.
–Jeremiah 29:13 AMP

As a young child, I longed to know God. And I did everything I knew to find this God who seemed so elusive.

Meditations, Mantras, and Offerings

My maternal grandmother was a Buddhist. She focused more on the meditation precepts, yet she still gave alms and obeisance to the monks and daily worshipped morning and night at the statue of Buddha, offering food, water, and incense, counting her beads, and praying aloud in a chant.

I would go to the monastery with her every week and sometimes even more often, joining her in concentrating on every breath that went in and out of my body or in every step or movement I made. I tried to emulate and imitate the mantras and the meditations in my search for truth and a living God.

Devout as she was, my grandmother knew only what had been passed down to her and was not able to point me to the peace of God I sought so desperately.

"May May Gyi, why is meditation not helping me find the answers to why I am here and where I am going? How do good deeds help you to have a better life in your next existence? Has anyone come back after they die? I keep repeating all these mantras and doing my beads, but what do they do? Who is hearing this, and who is looking? I am offering food every day to the statue of Buddha. Will he eat and drink? Is there a god inside of him?"

Innumerable Gods and No Answers

On the other hand, my paternal grandmother believed in numerous gods. She was surely the originator of the dark side of my frantic desire as an impressionable child to please these gods. She not only believed in the Buddhist god, the Lord Gautama, who was originally an Indian prince that had searched for truth and found Nirvana, but she also believed in the Hindu god Ganesh, the elephant statue with many hands, who was the family god inherited down through the generations on my grandfather's side.

"Phwa Phwa, why do you have two gods? Which god is more powerful? Does grandfather also believe like you do? Why does he say that when he dies, he will be cremated and his ashes thrown into the Ganges River? I don't see him pray or go to the temple. Does he not want to go with you?" To all my questions, she only nodded. I was not as close to her as I was to Mummy's mother. There was something otherworldly about her.

We also had the *nats*, the spirits—whether good or evil, I did not know—who I was told lived in the trees outside our home and elsewhere in the dark woods. "Phwa Phwa, you said there are spirits everywhere I look, but I don't see any of them. The only thing I see at night are dozens of candles lit at every stair corner and in every nook and cranny. And why are little platforms built into the trees where we have to offer food and water?" She just shook her head and walked past me.

Superstitions were rife. "Don't let down your hair, especially at night, because a demon might attach itself to your hair." Balls of fire, the hooting of owls, black cats, and other taboos all heralded the presence of spirits lurking in the unseen dark. Utterly entrenched in my mind was a frightening scene I once witnessed while with my grand aunt—five women with glazed eyes danced in a drunken frenzied orgy around a circle of firelight. "What are they doing? Why do their eyes look so glassy?" I never received a satisfying answer.

The Quest for Truth

To this inquisitive soul, the longing to know God from a very young age was very strong, and I visited the monasteries with my maternal grandmother and took part in all the duties of lighting candles and offering water and food to the statues of the Buddha as well as to the monks. I sat in a pious fashion with both legs under me as I followed their chanting, trying to imitate my grandmother. "What are they saying, May May Gyi? I don't know the words."

"Just listen, Ni Ni, it will come to you."

My paternal grandmother frequented a Hindu temple. The sights and sounds and smells terrified me. I would enter those dark-curtained doors with her, bracing myself as the cloying perfume of the heavy incense and the smell of sacrificed fruit assailed my nostrils. "I can't see, Phwa Phwa. Will they light more candles?" She seemed not to hear me. I religiously followed their rituals, gingerly placing the "sacred" ash on my forehead and chanting their droning prayers. With her rigorous keeping of the worship traditions passed down to her, she only caused me to be afraid, which heightened my struggle to appease angry, demanding gods.

At home, because I did not want to leave anything to chance, I made it my responsibility to take care of the morning and evening offerings to the statue of Buddha for both my grandmothers. I took this good deed, or *thadu*, upon myself, as none of my three sisters truly understood or wanted to take part in religious activities.

Having been brought up as a child in this strong religious setting and as the product of an unequally yoked marriage between two people who had never known the unconditional love and warmth of their parents, I spent my formative years asking the age-old queries: "Who am I?" "Why am I here?" And, "Where am I going when I die?"

The Pivotal Turn

Forever etched in my memory is a twilight evening on my fourteenth birthday that became the pivotal turn in my journey as I searched for something or someone for whom my heart so longed but still did not know.

Alone in the prayer room, separated from the rest of the house, I can still see myself: eyes closed, head bowed, kneeling in prayer before the statue of Buddha. "Awegatha, Awegatha, Awegatha; Kayagan, Wasigan, Manawgan, Kapadawtha, Khupthein thaw a pyit twe go. . . ."

The previous morning I had brought this god I worshipped a bowl of steaming rice, little sweet cakes, and a small glass of water. I had come that evening to give obeisance and to take away the morning offering.

Vividly and clearly, as if it were yesterday, I looked up into the face of what had always been a peaceful-looking Buddha. But that fateful evening, I imagined that it was smiling at me. Into my mind crept the words my friend Celina had uttered just the previous day when she had strangely warned me, "Nita, you need to think about dying."

"Why do I need to think about dying?" I asked.

But all Celina said was, "The Buddha you are worshipping will one day laugh at you."

Did he just smile? My thundering heart wondered. It was so real, but it was gone in a split second. Perhaps I had just imagined it, but that was enough for me. With my heart pounding, pulse racing, senses reeling, and every nerve jangling, I ran from the prayer room, never again to return with the same worshipping, seeking heart for a god I could not know.

I ran into the bedroom I shared with my sisters, and that night I crept under the covers and stayed there, shrouded by my white mosquito netting. It became a place I could safely hide because now I had no god to pray to who would protect and keep me safe during the long night.

What ensued following that frightening night was a fear that stifled and crippled me, holding me in bondage to what was unknown and unwanted, yet threatened me with demons that I felt were surrounding me and waiting for me to fall into their evil clutches. For two years, this unrelenting fear tormented me so much that nightfall became a nerve-wracking time. Bit by bit, the memory, though not eradicated, became a little faded, but fear was always in the wings, waiting to overpower and torment.

Why didn't I go to my mother? As a child, I figured I had no choice since Buddhism was the only religion accepted in our household, and she was not allowed to influence us with her foreign religion.

Finding No Answers

At night, questions would race through my head. My paternal granduncle had recently passed, and I heard that his ashes were taken to float down the river. Cremation and scattered ashes down the River Ganges had always been the family tradition, the custom chosen at the death of a loved one because of the belief this action signified.

Was it because the soul was now released? Were they floating to an eternal destination? One could not find out, for no one could return to give an answer. I had asked these questions myself, but it had been before I knew where I was going and whom I was going to be with when this life would finally end for me.

I asked the monks when I sojourned to the neighboring monastery time and again with my maternal grandmother during my childhood because

I was afraid to ask my father or grandparents. But no one, including the monks with their saffron robes, seemed to know the answer.

Reincarnation and Nirvana

"Ni Ni," a monk told me, "you will go through several reincarnations, coming back either as a human being or an animal. It is good to come back as a man, so you can reach the state of Nirvana and perhaps become a Buddha, but you have to do a lot of good deeds before you can reach this end point."

I had given obeisance to this monk as a child, but his answer did not satisfy my curious mind.

No one in my family seemed to ask questions or really care. Content to skim along the surface, life went on as usual. But my charmed life as I knew it would soon be shaken.

Part II

Love That Could Not Let Me Go

Chapter 12

Sweet Sixteen and Never Been Kissed

*We are torn between a nostalgia for the familiar
and an urge for the foreign and strange.
As often as not, we are homesick most
for the places we have never known.
—Carson McCullers[1]*

1960, Rangoon, Burma

In my sixteenth year, I graduated from Methodist English High School. As I prepared for the day, Mummy held up my Burmese wrap-around skirt and long-sleeved blouse I had just brought in from the sewing table. "You are so tiny. You're only five-and-a-half-feet tall, and your waist is sixteen inches. Esme tells me that you only weigh eighty-six pounds."

"Well, Gail is five-feet-eleven inches, and she always teases me that you left part of me behind when you gave birth to me." We ended up laughing as we always did.

On graduation day, I walked across the stage, and my science teacher hugged me. Handing my certificates to me, she whispered, "Nita, I am so proud of you. You graduated with honors in physics and chemistry. I am told that you are going to Rangoon University and will be taking up science courses with a view to entering the engineering or medical school program, and I wish you all the best." My teachers had pushed me to excel, and I was indebted to them.

The Grand Surprise

After the awards, I returned to my seat, and Daddy handed me a fat manilla envelope. He and Mummy were beaming. "We have planned a special trip for you. Mummy and I will take you with us on our final home leave cruise to England."

"Oh, I can't wait! I love London. What about Esme, Gail, and Chicky?"

"No, this trip is just for you. They still have school, and you have worked so hard."

That trip has never left my memory because it made such an impact on my budding youth. To be able to travel all over England as a sixteen-year-old and be treated as an adult without having the responsibility of making sure my younger sisters were having a good time was such a delight to me.

On the ocean liner, I had young men standing at attention—pulling out my chair at dinner and attending to me everywhere I ventured. I tried not to let my cheeks flush with embarrassment or look bewildered at behavior and protocols I did not understand. In London, we stayed at a beautiful Victorian hotel where I had my own room and a high four-poster bed piled with satin cushions.

We saw the original *My Fair Lady* with Rex Harrison and Audrey Hepburn, *The Sound of Music*, *The King and I*, and other Rodgers & Hammerstein musicals, along with live concerts that featured Shirley Bassey,

Frank Sinatra, and the Platters. At times, they literally took my breath away. I immersed myself in the British history I loved as we visited many places I had voraciously studied in school. We rode double-decker buses, trams, and underground tubes. This highly imaginative sixteen-year-old took it all in, breathing in the romance and the pulse of the bustling city and then reveling in the lush meadows and foliage of the countryside.

My only regret was that there was no time to visit the well-renowned Sadler's Wells Ballet School, to which I had a letter of introduction from my ballet teacher who had studied there. To this day, my ten years of studying ballet have left me with an ongoing passion for gliding gracefully and continually practicing my arabesque, pirouette, and plie in my sanctuary spaces, as I had become so accustomed to posture and grace.

Secret Yearnings

This was my heritage, this extreme lap of luxury. I could not want for more, yet something deep inside me was still searching. A yearning for something more that I could not see—something that seemed elusive and far out of my reach. In the back of my mind was a garden, beautiful and ethereal. Would I ever find it?

Barely sixteen and having just returned from the trip that left me starry-eyed, but strangely enough still searching, I was almost losing hope of finding this place.

I started my studies at the university and made new friends. But I still could not put aside the secret yearnings of my heart to find what I could not fathom but continued to seek.

Yet an unseen hand was moving in my life. I did not know that I would soon be put on a path with a young medical student whose future would intertwine with mine and move me from a world full of riches that could never satisfy my seeking heart to a life of less that would, ironically, bring me satisfaction and fulfillment.

Little did I know that when my daddy gave Esme and me permission to go to a university group three-day water festival and Burmese New Year party, a very first in our overprotected lives, this unseen hand would have me meet a shy young man who would become my forever husband and draw me closer to what my seeking heart longed for.

Chapter 13

Two Hearts Beating as One

Two souls with but a single thought, two hearts that beat as one!
-John Keats[1]

I was barely 16 and you were not yet 20,
when you came into my life, and I was changed forever.
We were both so shy, yet something bigger than ourselves
drew us to each other, and we have never let go.
–Nita Tin[2]

April 13, 1960, Rangoon, Burma.

I was sixteen when I met a sweet, gentle man who had not yet turned twenty. That day would prove to be the turning point of my life in my search for meaning.

Anticipating the fun of the year's *Thingyan*, I got up early that morning. Festivities had been happening the entire week, and now Daddy allowed me to join in. The Burmese New Year was being ushered in by three days of the religious water festival, *Thingyan*, that marked the old year going out and the new year coming in. There was traditional dancing, singing, and cultural shows along with religious activities of the Theravada Buddhism pagodas and monasteries.

As part of the cleansing ritual to welcome each new year, the age-old custom was to sprinkle water with a laurel branch on one another as a sign of respect, blessing, and good wishes. But with this celebration falling during the hottest month in Southeast Asia, people young and old alike would end up dousing strangers and passersby in boisterous merriment.

Our experience of *Thingyan* as children and in our early teens was to soak each other with buckets of water outside our house in the garden. But this year, my sister and I had been invited to the water festival by Ko Tu, a law school student related by marriage to my family. Daddy agreed to let us go with the injunction that Esme and I stay together.

The day arrived, and our chauffeur watched us get into the big open truck that would take us around the city so we could get water thrown at us. We were the first to arrive, and I got into the truck and sat down right behind the driver's seat. A tall, slim young man climbed into the front and sat beside the driver.

I Know You

What happened next amused me. A girl I knew from my school quickly got in beside him, and he continued to stare straight ahead. Then the driver got down to check the tires, and while the girl was looking out of the window and waving at a friend, this young man elegantly and quickly slid out the driver's side and jumped down from the truck.

Soon, people were climbing onto the truck, and the driver started the engine. Before I knew it, this guy slipped into the back and came to where I was sitting, wedged between the driver's seat and a stack of towels. He picked up the towels and asked if he could sit there. I said yes and moved over to let him sit behind the driver's seat. Very quietly, he sat and looked out the front. He was just as shy as I was.

As the truck began moving, he turned around and said, "I'm Pe. I am a medical student."

"Oh, I am Nita. I am in my first year at the university."

"I know you," he said shyly. "I saw you a couple of years ago near the Su'le Pagoda. I was driving by, and you were walking to your car with your mother. You had two long pigtails."

Soon the truck pulled out amidst loud clapping and cheering. We passed decorated stations on the side of the road loaded with things to eat and drink. Pretty girls carrying silver bowls were throwing flower-scented water on passersby. Some of the men got down to sample the food, while others took bowls of water and gently poured it on the girls serving them.

I Will Shield You

We entered the city, where revelers with fire hoses were ready to douse the trucks that passed by. A few boys winked at each other. I quickly learned that this was the time for the boys to shield the girls with the towels they had around their necks. The water started spraying fast and furious, and I had to take gulps of air between the unexpected assaults of water from the fire hoses.

I sucked in air, trying to balance myself. By this time, we were all standing in the now-stationary truck, hiding our faces from the onslaught. What happened next was sweet.

"Are you alright?" Pe steadied me while he shielded me with his thick towel. "You can turn your face into my shoulder so you can breathe." He turned me gently away from the direction of the water that was being pumped into the open truck.

Breathe? My face was against his shoulder. I could hear the pounding of his heart. *Breathe, Nita, breathe!* I had never been that close to a boy before. Never had muscular arms around my slight body. Never breathed in a hint of gentle aftershave and mint toothpaste in such close quarters.

Each day of that festival, we sat down in the same place on the bus, and each day he stood up to shield me from the water blasts. There was something gentle about him.

The long-awaited New Year's Eve party was on the last day of the water festival. Esme and I were at a childhood friend's house getting ready, changing out of our wet clothes. Daddy had given us till midnight to return home.

Aye came into our room with towels. "Get ready for the evening. It will be a whole night of dancing." After I showered quickly and changed, I went downstairs to peek into the huge living room where the dancing would take place.

Two Hearts Strangely Drawn Together

As I quietly walked down one side of the steps, at the same time, Pe was coming down the other. "You are very pretty," he said awkwardly.

A little embarrassed, I said, "Who said so?"

Equally embarrassed, he looked away. "Everyone says so! Guys from the engineering college tell me that they go and wait outside your classes just to catch a glimpse of you."

I looked down at my toes.

We were both so shy, yet something bigger than ourselves drew us to each other. Little did either of us know our lives would mesh that night as we brought in a new year. Two timid hearts would be drawn together. And they would grow to beat as one.

The music began playing as the room started slowly filling up, and energetic partners jived, rock 'n' rolled, and did the cha-cha and the twist. Soon the dance floor was packed. The song "Unchained Melody" came on, and the dancers slowed to either a waltz or slow dance.

"Will you dance with me?" Pe took my hand, and we moved in time with the music.

I'll Remember Tonight

We were quiet as we danced rather stiffly. Then, slowly, we began to get closer as the music became more intimate. "Remember When" was being crooned by the Platters. When Pat Boone's voice came on, the words from "I'll Remember Tonight" struck a chord in our hearts, and we joined in, softly humming to the tune.

By the time the song ended, the top of my head was leaning against his cheek, his left hand had pulled my hand gently on his chest, and we both felt safe and comfortable as we kept in time with the music. Even with my super-high heels, my head just came up to his chest, and I loved the sweetness of his gesture, bending a little so he could hold me close.

Out of the corner of my eye, I saw Aye dancing with someone she had been sitting beside on the water festival truck the last three days. Something was happening to them too. We all seemed to be floating on air.

After a short break, a live band came on, and my heart pounded as the soloist sang what was taking place in my heart. "Why do I feel this way?" she crooned. "It seems there are butterflies in my tummy. He is holding me close and feeling the same way."

We danced to the beat as he held me gently, and my head softly rested on his chest. I felt an indescribable peace. I felt his gentle strength. I felt as though we were one. As the band played continuously, we danced and danced and danced and danced.

The Beginning of a Journey

The music stopped for another break, and we walked out to the veranda under a starry night. We sat on a couch, and he held me close. He nestled me in the crook of his arm, and I slowly leaned my head on his broad shoulders. I seemed to belong there. We talked softly until the music started back again. Elvis Presley's rendering of "I Can't Help Falling in Love" came next, and through every song, we continued dancing together, oblivious of everyone around us, until it was time to go. And then we parted reluctantly.

That night as I lay at home in bed, I knew this was the beginning of a journey. Where, I did not know. But Pe and I were both certain that evening that we were meant to be together. I was strangely drawn to this person I had been with for only three days. There was something different about him, something I could not put a handle on. One thing that warmed me from within was when He spoke gently and trustingly about a God who had always led his steps. When I asked if he felt that his God had led him to medical school, he said, "Yes, I pray each night and read my Bible, and I know His plans are good. The Bible says if I trust Him with all my heart, and if I acknowledge Him as the One who knows what is best for me, He will direct my path."

I wanted to ask him how he knew this to be true, but we would have more time together, and I would find out. I had never met anyone like him before. There was something solid about him. I had no way of knowing that the God I had long been searching for was laying a path for me, according to the plan He had for me, with the person He had designed for me.

I certainly had no idea there was a God who cared for me and was orchestrating situations and circumstances that would lead me to the answers I was seeking. And it never entered my mind that the heart of this sheltered Burmese girl brought up by doting, wealthy parents was about to be renewed.

Chapter 14

Cloud Nine, Double Dating, and University Days

How do I love thee? Let me count the ways.
I love thee to the depth and breadth and height my soul can reach,
when feeling out of sight for the ends of being and ideal grace.
–Elizabeth Barrett Browning[1]

And we know that in all things God works
for the good of those who love him,
who have been called according to his purpose.
–Romans 8:28 NIV

The next day, my friend Aye and I excitedly exchanged notes about the party. "I saw you dancing with Victor, Aye! You were looking up at him, and I saw how you looked into each other's eyes."

"And I saw how you and Pe couldn't keep your eyes off each other. That night was awesome! I can't wait to see Vic again. Isn't it funny that both he and Pe are in medical school?"

Aye looked so happy. "Can you imagine us being doctors' wives?"

"I can, Aye. There was just something magical for both you and me last night. It would be wonderful if we lived close together like we do now, once you and I get married to them. We could look after each other's kids."

"I asked Vic about Pe to make sure he comes from a good family. I want my friend to have the best."

"What did he say about Pe?" In Burmese high society, family background was very important. Education also played a meaningful role, with parents hoping their children would excel and choose careers in the medical, legal, and engineering fields.

"Well, Nita, Vic said that Pe's father is a lawyer. He is also the minister of land records and settlement. His mother was a lawyer too, but he lost her when he was about thirteen years old."

"Oh, that is so sad. He must miss his mother very much!"

"Vic said Pe's older brother, Patrick, is practicing at Rangoon General Hospital and specializes in ophthalmology. He trained at a hospital in Cincinnati, Ohio. His sister is working at the United Nations office in New York and has a very high-ranking position as a UNDP officer. He says he is Patricia's contemporary and that he knows their family well."

"I wish I could have met Pe's sister while she lived here. He said she is five years older than him and always took care of him. When he was about six years old, she beat up a boy who tried to steal his lunch. She's been like a mother to him since their May May died. Pe also told me that his mother took her barrister's exam when he was not yet in kindergarten, and he sat by her side and held the inkpot for her fountain pen."

I couldn't stop talking about Pe. "Daddy told me that they come from a line of one of the Burmese kings. Isn't that amazing? Daddy said that his father had racehorses, and they rode bareback, and his mother was an accomplished horsewoman. He also said that Patrick was the darling of the upcoming crowd and that he was chosen to escort the Queen's cousin, Princess Alexandria of Kent, when she visited Burma."

I giggled as I thought of Pe's brother, whom I had previously met when he examined my eyes, telling me I had "high myopia" and needed glasses. I never knew until I was in the sixth grade why I couldn't see the leaves on the trees. He was six foot three inches and had the figure of Apollo and the looks and education that classified him as the most eligible bachelor. I whispered to Aye, "I heard that the nurses all love him, and they run out to wave at him when he drives by in his white convertible. But his younger brother is the one I would run out and wave to."

"I feel the same way about Vic," Aye gushed, and soon we were in deep conversation about Vic and his accomplishments and charm. "He is the one for me. I knew it when he looked into my eyes. They were so gentle and loving."

"And oh, Pe told me later that Ko Tu told him at the party not to toy with my affections because I was very sheltered and came from a good family."

We laughed so hard that tears were rolling down our cheeks.

Innocent Dreamers Always Chaperoned

My father, who brought us up in the strict Burmese fashion of those days, allowed Pe and me to meet only when we were chaperoned. So for the first year we knew each other, my oldest sister was always with us. A year into our courtship, we were finally allowed to date. Still, if we went out for an evening meal, it was always with three other couples; they became our lifelong friends. Out of those four couples, three of the pairs got married.

All three of us girls were born in the same year, and our weddings also fell within a year.

Those were idyllic days. Most weekends, we danced at parties in the evening or rode in Pe's jeep down to the jetty at the Rangoon River, where we ate outdoors. We'd find the biggest round table at the prettiest spot. The food came in baskets lined with red-checkered wax paper, and each couple would share their meal using paper plates and plasticware and drinking from tall paper cups.

The end of each meal was always hilarious. Without fail, Pe would collect all the serving baskets and finish off any remaining food. This was a standing joke. "Hey, Pe. Do you want our chicken? I bet you can't eat any more." Pe was so slim and tall. Where did he hide all that food?

Afterward, we'd stroll along the promenade, hand in hand and heart to heart. Most evenings, we would gaze at the sunset across the river. Hues of gold and red and bright orange would linger and then slowly fade away amid the sounds of waves lapping against the jetty and seagulls squawking. Then the moon would rise against the darkened sky. What could be more glorious?

Young hearts, young lives, arms entwined, heads touching, dreaming innocent dreams, unaware of the drama that would soon play out and disperse each couple in separate directions. Reluctantly we would all pile into Pe's jeep and say goodbye as we arrived at our respective homes.

Choices

We started to date when I was in my first year at Rangoon University. My classes were at the Intermediate Center of Arts and Science, where I majored in physics, chemistry, and mathematics.

Pe was interested in my choice of subjects. "What made you decide what to study?"

"I always get excited about algebraic equations and the end results of mathematical problems, and physics and chemistry were my strong subjects. I knew I was not cut out to dissect and learn the inner organs and mechanical workings of insects and mammals, so I guess my choice was easy."

After the two-year course at the Intermediate College of Arts and Science, students in the mathematics section could compete for placement in engineering, and students in the biology section for medical school. As it turned out, I transferred to biology and ended up placing thirteenth in the nation for a place in medical school.

When I told my parents that I would not be going to medical school, Daddy's face fell. "Tita, so you don't want to be a doctor?"

"No, I decided to change my major to English Literature and Language. I will be studying poetry, drama, linguistics, phonetics, and the teaching of English as a second language."

Mummy understood. "She loves reading and writing. I think she will be very happy with her choices."

Pe had only two more years in medical school, after which we planned to marry. He grinned when I whispered, "Darling, I decided that you could be the physician and surgeon, and I will take care of our home, and we will have a beautiful family."

I was thankful that Pe had helped me in my decision as I struggled to make up my mind if I should transfer. "Think about what you love and what you want to do when you leave uni."

"It's crazy because I spent the last two years in the sciences. I feel that I have wasted my time."

"Nothing is wasted. There is no end to learning, and everything we learn makes up who we are. Look at how you scored thirteenth in the nation for a place in medical school. That is something to be proud of. All the things you have learned will be useful in the life we have together when you become my wife. God is in the business of working all things out for our good and His glory. I will be praying for you." He hugged me, his eyes smiling so sweetly into mine.

Pe knew I needed help processing my jumbled thoughts and emotions. He taught me how much we lose out when we don't stop and pay attention to the heart's prompting. I had never before stopped long enough to do that—to give attention to who I really was and who I wanted to be. But now, here was someone who listened and made me pay attention—lovingly, kindly, gently.

"You do love reading," he said. "I've seen your library, and I know you are probably the only one who makes use of it, you little bookworm."

"I know. I do love English literature. Remember the time I told you how Esme grabbed the book I was reading and threw it from the veranda into the flower beds? I chased after her, and she ran crying to tell Mummy that I was going to get her, without explaining that she started it."

"Reading meant so much to you."

"Yes, it was my way of escape. As a child and all through my teen years, I read book after book, devouring encyclopedias and even studying the dictionary. At night, we had lights out at 9 p.m., but Daddy would find me hours later in the bathroom still reading because I could not put my book down."

He looked at me with those tender eyes, and my heart melted. Pe had to be the one my soul had always longed for. With him, there was none of the loneliness or lostness that had consumed me. Instead, I felt a oneness with him—like Elizabeth Barrett Browning, whose poems touched my heart. If Pe had asked me how much I loved him, I would gladly quote:

> *How do I love thee? Let me count the ways.*
> *I love thee to the depth and breadth and height*
> *My soul can reach, when feeling out of sight*
> *For the ends of being and ideal grace.*[2]

Chapter 15

The Swinging of the Pendulum

The pendulum swings its wide arch, cutting through the air
with threatening strokes. Its sharp blade is ever present
and always moving closer in arks of fear.
The pit lies below in dark, endless depths of nothingness.
Its cry is one of forever and silence.
–Lynn MacKinnon[1]

There is a time for everything,
and a season for every activity under the heavens:
a time to be born and a time to die,
a time to plant and a time to uproot,
a time to kill and a time to heal,
a time to tear down and a time to build,
a time to weep and a time to laugh,
a time to mourn and a time to dance,
a time to scatter stones and a time to gather them,
a time to embrace and a time to refrain from embracing,
a time to search and a time to give up,
a time to keep and a time to throw away,
a time to tear and a time to mend,
a time to be silent and a time to speak,
a time to love and a time to hate,

a time for war and a time for peace.
−Ecclesiastes 3:1–8 NIV

Rangoon, in its heyday, was peaceful and prosperous. Then, sadly, the dictatorship military regime brought the whole country to its knees in an insidious, revolutionary march to make her a socialist nation.

On March 2, 1962, General Ne Win, a Burmese general and political leader, seized power in a military-staged coup d'état. We lost our parliamentary government, the constitution was taken away, and we no longer had rights.

Burma, my beloved country, became a land where fear reigned, and joy and freedom had been snatched away by a despotic military dictator.

"Tita, make sure your sisters don't say anything negative about the government over the phone. Our lines are being tapped by military intelligence. I was at a ship's party, and military intelligence servicemen were everywhere."

The telephone rang just then. Daddy picked up the phone. "Ohn residence."

"Hello, George. This is Rose. Eric has just been taken away in handcuffs. They said he would be put in prison. They said he helped Tom escape." She was sobbing. "They also took old Dr. Sawhan for questioning because Tom escaped in his car."

"I am so sorry, Rose. Eve and I will come right over."

"No, don't come, George. Our house is being watched."

Word-of-mouth sharing was guarded. We had no freedom of speech. The dance parties and friendly gatherings continued as usual, but there always seemed to be several elephants in the room, and the spark had gone. Underground news traveled fast as more civilians were taken, and some seemed to have disappeared without a trace. Innocent people were being tortured, imprisoned, or even killed without trial. Uncle Eric was put in solitary confinement and given a long sentence without any representation.

Was there a God? If so, why did He allow this to happen?

Chapter 16

Massacre in the Student Union Building

"They shoot in the head, but they don't know revolution dwells in the heart."

For many people on the ground in Myanmar, lines such as
"with what grief I will grieve for you, my martyred son"
by [the poet] A Phaw Khaing have become daily reality.
People who are at a loss for words tend to find answers in poetry...

Many will remember Khet Thi by one of his famous lines,
written in response to military violence:
"You try so hard to bury us underground,
because you don't know that we are the seeds."[1]

July 7, 1962

Starkly illuminated in my memories of that July day in 1962 were friends who were gunned down at the university by the ruthless military dictator government while we hid in the campus library at the Arts and Science Building.

A professor, fearing for our safety, shouted out, "Listen, everyone! Get into the ladies' common room and stay there until I tell you to come out!"

Much shouting was accompanied by frightened screams and pandemonium.

Our friend Peter was the last to burst into the library just before the professor locked the door. "I saw dozens of military police cars surround the campus and dozens more military cars following them. They started to spray tear gas at the unarmed students." He stopped and took a deep breath. "From where I was hiding in the bushes behind the library, it looked to me like more than a thousand soldiers from the Number 4 Battalion took position around the student union building, armed with G-3 rifles. They stormed into the building from all sides, and for thirty minutes, they shot the students in rapid succession."

Another friend, Bobby, was hysterical. "Arthur was shot down. We had just come back from rowing and heard the commotion. You know how tall he was. His legs were broken by a heartless soldier so that the crude coffin could accommodate his six feet two-inch body."

It broke our hearts.

The sounds of terror, the blood spattered on the walls of the student union hall, and the lifeless bodies of friends thrown into makeshift coffins still haunt me.

We also learned of the awful follow-up of this senseless shooting. The news had spread even though the government had tried to suppress it. We were told that parents were not allowed to identify their children. Halls of learning were closed for several months as the government tried to cover up the bloody massacre of innocent students at Rangoon University. And despite government suppression, to this day, July 7, 1962, is still commemorated as a day never to be forgotten.

The horror and the grief in the aftermath. The sound of the assault rifles. The smell of smoke. The ensuing months when we could not return to the university. All these atrocities were committed by a powerful military government bent on a socialist propaganda.

Lord, Please Protect Her

As though it were yesterday, I can still hear Pe's gentle voice whispering in my ear as he came to pick me up from the university as soon as he could. "I was praying for you, Darling. I love you so much."

I was shaking and sobbing uncontrollably.

He held me close. "I was so worried. We could hear the shots all the way from the lab where we were having practical session classes at the med school. They said they could even hear it from across Inya Lake." He held me closer, "Are you all right, Darling? I know it was such a shock to you being right there so close to the shooting."

"I'm okay, but it was so awful. We were so scared. Our professors shooed us into the ladies' common room, and they locked us in so we would not get hurt. Our biology professor was so brave. She went to see if there were any other students or teachers so she could bring them safely into the LCR. Our math professor did the same. The noise was awful, awful. I don't think I will ever get it out of my mind."

"Sweetheart, I am so glad you are safe." He held me tightly. "The Lord answered my prayer, and He protected you."[2]

I was still shaking, my words barely a whisper, "I can't believe Arthur and some of our friends are dead."

He stroked my hair and wiped my tears. "Try to put it out of your mind."

I shuddered as I shook my head. "I can't."

You'll Never Walk Alone

At my home, Pe got up and walked across our living room. He took a record from the case he was carrying and placed it on the player in the corner.

"Listen to this song. It tells about Jesus holding us close until the storm passes by." I listened to the words of that beautiful song that has since become one of my favorites, "Hold Me Close Till the Storm Passes By."[3]

A peace came over me as we sat quietly together. I whispered into his ear, "I wish I knew your Jesus."

"You will. I am praying every day that He will become your Savior too."

With a quick hug, Pe got up and went to the record player again. He put on a different record and pulled me up onto my feet. As he began to dance with me, Elvis Presley's rendering of "You'll Never Walk Alone" streamed through our living room. Pe smiled his sweet smile. "It's going to be all right."

I looked up at him. He looked as though he was about to say something, but he stopped when he saw Daddy walk into the room to pick up his briefcase.

Pe hesitated as Daddy left the room, then whispered, "Your father told me the other day that he hoped that as a Buddhist, you would carry on the family tradition."

Pe had to be careful. But I wanted to be like him. I wanted what he had. He seemed to be filled with something that was so tangible and comforting yet so otherworldly. Out of him flowed love, joy, peace, patience, kindness, goodness, faithfulness, gentleness, and self-control, which I later learned was the fruit of a Spirit-filled life. My heart longed for a life like his. His trust in a sovereign God who loved him with an unconditional love and whom he addressed as his heavenly Father was something I did not have. And I wanted it more than all my earthly wealth.

Chapter 17

My Forever Soul Mate

So different, yet in our sameness
of soul and spirit and mind, we have pooled our life
until the boundaries of two different lives enmesh and swirl together
forming one complete whole.
−Nita Tin[1]

Despite the horrors and circumstances, life went on as it always does. We studied, took exams, and spent all our spare time together. Except for the political climate and the insidious changes going on around us, life for the social elite did not change much.

We had our dance parties in our own houses. We rock n' rolled, danced the cha-cha and the twist, and let out our energy in an environment that was safe and comfortable. Within those walls, there was hope. There was positivity, fun, and laughter. Nothing could dampen the spirits of these young socialites who had grown up with the frivolity and fun that often accompanies living in freedom and security.

I loved the impromptu gatherings. These moments were unforgettable as couples danced or stood holding hands under the star-studded sky.

However, for those several years younger than us, all this would be taken away as life in our surroundings drastically changed. But for the moment, that was far away. And pursuing graduate and post-graduate learning and balancing intense study with living life was still the norm.

Big Rooster

"Darling, I'll pick you up as soon as I get through the hospital rounds. Mr. Matthews is having a party at his house, and all our group will be there."

Dressed in a white brocade wraparound I had quickly stitched that afternoon and topped with a red velvet *aingyi*, I greeted Pe when he came, and the delighted look in his eyes was enough.

When we arrived, the house was lit, the doors and mullioned windows were open, and the music was welcoming as we poured into Mr. Matthews' huge living room.

"Hey, Thu Ye Aung Sein, good to see you, man."

"Hi, Aye and Vic. Glad you made it. We're going to have so much fun."

"Mr. Matthews, thank you for opening up your home."

Pe had been immediately dubbed *Kyet Kyee*, the Burmese equivalent for Big Rooster, because he had eaten a whole chicken at our first four-couple date night out. Nicknames like this were given in love and merriment.

As we danced to the rhythm of the slower music, Pe acquired another name. Oblivious of the bright lights on us as we held each other close, someone yelled out "Bo Lin Htin," the Burmese equivalent of Captain Brilliance. Laughing, he whispered that he didn't care who was watching. Dancing with me was his slice of heaven on earth.

Names like *Pah Moent Gyi* (Big Loaf of Bread), *Bear Kin* (Peking Duck), and *A Yoe Ba Dei Thah* (Skeleton) stuck for life and were so much a part of cherished friends feeling comfortable in their affection and love for one another.

Utopian Days

I loved attending Pe's tennis matches and watching as he played single, doubles, or mixed doubles. Tennis was a big part of his life. "Daddy is a national tennis champ," he told me. "And in the days when it was an all-white tennis club, he was a very popular guest despite being a Burmese national. He trained all three of us. Ko Patrick and Ma Ma Pat are national champs; both have won so many trophies."

I was so excited when Pe won the university and inter-state tennis competitions. "Darling, you are awesome. You won 6-0, 6-0 both times." He put his arms around me and grinned. His love for the game was unmistakable.

After two years of double dating, we were finally allowed to go to the movies just by ourselves. By then, Daddy trusted Pe enough to let us date on our own. We had so many fun moments. We spent summer evenings swimming at the Kokine Club and taking long drives along beautiful Inya Lake, where we sat on benches and watched the sunset. We loved our time together, cooking with his dad at his house on Thayagone Street, Insein, or just having long, cozy chats at home with my family.

It was also a time of serious talks, many of them about our studies, our families, and our future life together. We would meander along the university paths and sometimes just drive to the edge of Inya Lake. Sitting hand in hand together in the car, we would open our hearts to each other. Often we watched the moon come up. A warm and wonderful peace enveloped us during those times as we stayed still, always ending with Pe thanking his heavenly Father and asking Him to choose His path for us.

We still enjoyed the parties at friends' homes and loved the dancing and the social times with our close-knit group, but the times we could just sit and be close to each other were times I remember and cherish most.

University students were still the target of the government. Broad institutional reforms introduced by the 1964 University Education Act brought Burma's universities under strict government control and profoundly hampered open, cohesive student activism. The aftermath of the 1962 Rangoon University protests ushered in a new era of underground student activism in which open, mass-student involvement in national politics erupted, but at this time, it was only sporadic. We, on the other hand, concentrated on our studies and moved in a circle of friends who were intent on graduating.

Will You Marry Me?

In 1965, Pe received his MBBS/MD degree from the Institute of Medicine, Rangoon.

"Darling, I am so proud of you."

He hugged me to him, "Thank you, Sweetheart!" He looked intently at me. "We can be married soon, but I am being sent away to Sagaing, a township in middle Burma. I have been assigned a year of internship at a government post instead of at General Hospital."

We decided to wait to get married until Pe returned, but we got engaged before he left for his year's internship. It was a beautiful evening. This was Pe's last week in Rangoon. We were dancing after a candlelit dinner at the members-only Pegu Club. Daddy had made the reservations for us, and the hostess had given us a little corner table tucked away behind a palm tree. As we danced, we thought about the first night we fell in love and how much had happened since then.

"Darling, I am so thankful God gave me to you. You are the best thing that has happened in my life." He pulled me close and whispered in my ear. "I want to show you something."

We left the club, and he drove past Judson Chapel in the Rangoon University complex and turned down the lane leading to Inya Lake. The moon was full, and the water glistened with an ethereal beauty. A slight wind lifted the leaves in a soothing rustling sound.

Pe stopped the car and came around to help me out. "Let's walk alongside the lake. I want to remember this time with you." There was a hushed silence except for the whisper of the gently flowing water and the soft crunch of the leaves beneath our feet. He stopped at a bench, and we sat down, holding each other as we had done that first night. He held me close and kissed me and then got up, feeling for something in his breast pocket. My heart swelled as he got down on one knee, holding out his mother's ring—two lustrous pearls entwined in a setting of diamonds that glistened in the light of the moon. "Will you marry me and be my wife and let me take care of you for the rest of our lives together?"

"Oh, Darling, that's all I want. You are all I ever wished for."

Three days later, Daddy threw a lovely party at our home in celebration. It was a quiet evening with just our two families, including Mummy's sister and her family—Aunty Mary, Uncle Robert, and my two young cousins, Christopher and Alexandria. They were emigrating to Perth in Western Australia, so this was also a time to wish them goodbye.

The next morning, we were at the train station as I was seeing Pe off for his year in Sagaing. "Write to me, Darling." I was teary-eyed as we held each other close. We had never been apart.

"I will." He held me closer. "I will come for you soon."

I hugged him back, "I am going to be so lonely without you."

He tried to make me smile, "It won't be long. I will take leave to be with you on your graduation day."

The train whistle started. We hugged each other close, and he kissed me tenderly, then jumped on the moving train, and we waved until we could no longer see each other.

I Saw You

The year was 1966. Pe was still in Sagaing. I was about to graduate after four years at the university, and we would be married soon. The ceremony for the University of Rangoon graduates would be held in the auditorium of Judson Chapel. Named after Adoniram Judson, the first American missionary to Burma, who translated the Burmese Bible and compiled the first Burmese-English dictionary, the building remains a historic landmark.

I graduated *cum laude* with a Bachelor of Arts degree. I had tied for first place in the nation with another classmate in my B.A., English Honors. He and I were chosen to represent the military regime as Burma's bright young stars, *Lu Ye Chun*. But ever-present in the back of my mind was that awful day during my first year at the university. I declined because I wanted no part of the Socialist indoctrination, but he accepted and went on to be a foreign ambassador for Burma.

The commencement started, but Pe was not in the auditorium. My parents were there, but the seat next to them was empty. I came onto the stage, a little disappointed that Pe had not kept his promise. My professor put my graduation stole on me, and I received my roll of honor and diploma.

As I came down from the stage, I stared in amazement. Pe's bearded face smiled at me through the grated window. He was wearing a leather jacket and looked somewhat travel-weary, but he had a big smile on his face. It looked like he had hurried from Sagaing to be there for me. Afterward, he was waiting for me in the parking lot near Daddy's car.

"Congratulations, Darling. I am so proud of you."

He held me in a big bear hug and gave me a huge bunch of pink roses. He did not smell of that wonderful fresh aftershave that I had been used to, and he didn't seem to have showered, but I was overjoyed to see him.

"Where have you been, Darling? You didn't come in time for my graduation."

"Oh, but I did. I saw the whole ceremony from start to finish. I was looking through the grate the whole time."

He grinned. "There was a men's doubles tennis championship tournament in Sagaing. Albert and I entered it, and we won first place. Look at my cup! I thought I would get back home in time, but the boat took longer than expected, and the train I rode on couldn't get here fast enough, so I borrowed Albert's bike and rode straight here. I saw you come up on the stage; my heart was pounding when I saw my beautiful, smart, and lovely little sweetheart win first place."

He gave me another hug while Daddy looked on, shaking his head. Mummy was smiling. She really loved Pe. Both of my parents were very fond of him.

"I hope you are coming to your wedding," Daddy joked.

Pe laughed. "I think so!"

He left right after, as it was a long journey back to Sagaing, and he had to report back to work early the next morning. I was grateful he had made that tiring trip to be with me even briefly.

Chapter 18

Two Wedding Ceremonies and a Longing for More

It was but a little that I passed from them,
but I found him whom my soul loveth:
I held him, and would not let him go,
until I had brought him into my mother's house,
and into the chamber of her that conceived me.
–Song of Solomon 3:4 KJV

The minute I heard my first love story I started looking for you,
Not knowing how blind that was. Lovers don't finally meet somewhere,
They're in each other all along.
–Rumi[1]

March 4, 1967, the day of our wedding finally arrived. After nearly seven years of waiting until he got his medical doctorate, Pe and I would become husband and wife. At 11 p.m. the previous night, I sewed the finishing touches to the afternoon outfit I would wear to the church wedding. I always finished at the very last minute, and Mummy was laughing and exclaiming, "Nita, you are going to be late for your funeral!" But the flurry of wedding preparations had died down, and everything was in order.

I was excited about the short ceremony that was to take place at Pe's family home church. As a Buddhist, I wondered if it would make me feel different. I knew that Pe was who he was because of his trust in Jesus.

Where Are You Going?

It was my last night at home, Mummy sat nearby, reading her Bible while I put the finishing touches on my long wedding veil. She watched me gather one end and sew on the tiny tiara that would hold it together at the top of my head.

"You always work into the night till you finish whatever you are doing, but you are always on time. I am going to miss our special times together."

I smiled. "You and Daddy and the girls can always come to visit us."

At that moment, Daddy came in. He glanced at my two suitcases near the corner of the room. "Where are you going, Tita?" He had not yet been able to bring himself to face the thought that I would be going away with Pe. My life as a physician and surgeon's wife in a remote village would begin as soon as we returned from our honeymoon.

"I am getting married, Daddy. I told you I would follow Pe to Palai." He looked crushed. Poor Daddy! He just could not reconcile in his mind that someone else would be taking care of me.

They said goodnight and went to bed. I sewed the last row of sequins to my long organza veil and smiled. This was my secret yearning. I was still a Buddhist, but I had always dreamed of wearing white and getting married in a church. And as I sewed, my thoughts swirled around. We would be repeating sacred vows to each other. Would I become totally one with him in spirit?

The Buddhist Ceremony

Pe and Alwyn, his best man, had slept over at our city apartment the night before to be on time for the Burmese Wedding Ritual at 6 a.m. This was Daddy's wise idea. "Now, Alwyn, make sure you wake Pe up at 5 a.m. We don't want him to be late."

Early morning came, and the two of us sat on a carpeted floor before a monk and in the presence of our families and close friends. As a Buddhist, I bowed my head in obeisance to the monk. Pe, as a Christian, participated in all the proceedings and was very respectful, but he just sat up straight, not bowing to the monks.

We simultaneously poured water into an ornamental silver bowl to signify two lives pooled together while the monk chanted blessings in Pali (Sanskrit). In the Buddhist religion, this ceremony made us man and wife.

"Do you feel married, Darling?" I whispered. I'm not sure whether he shook his head or nodded.

The Christian Nuptials

The simple church ceremony followed at 2 p.m. and was officiated by the family pastor. My sister Esme was the maid of honor, and Alwyn was the best man. I wore the beautiful lacy white outfit I had made and bobby-pinned a huge white silk rose to the top of my head, from which my handmade veil floated. I carried a cluster of white roses and sprigs of lily of the valley tied with a white satin ribbon that fell in a graceful stream in front of my *hta mein*.

"You look gorgeous, my Darling! I love you so much."

"I love you too. I've waited so long for this day."

"Do you, Pe Than Tin, take this woman to be your lawfully wedded wife?" "Do you, Nita Ohn, take this man to be your lawfully wedded husband?" We repeated the short vows after the pastor and then signed the marriage license. So now, after the Christian ceremony, we were again proclaimed husband and wife.

I had thought that somehow this sacred church wedding would seal something spiritual in me, but I felt no different in my spirit. The nagging hole for something I longed for but did not know was still there. I quickly brushed away the thought. As Pe would say, "All in God's time."

"Do you feel married now, Darling?" I asked as we were chauffeured home.

"Of course, Sweetheart. You are my wife, my beloved, and I am yours."

He turned to hold me close. We could not kiss in public, especially in front of our driver, but Pe's closeness made me choke with so much love for this gentle, wonderful man who was now mine. From the very beginning, Pe and I had always been complete soul mates, and I was overcome with the thought that I was now joined totally and forever with the dearest man on earth to me.

My voice shook as I looked at the new golden band on my ring finger. I looked up at Pe. "You are my husband, my only beloved, and I am yours." My fingers entwined in his.

Nothing Is Too Much for You

This simple ceremony was followed by a lavish wedding reception at our country home, where five hundred guests were invited to a garden party replete with a seven-course formal dinner. Daddy had planned the sit-down dinner on the lawns and had booked a live band from 5 p.m. to 1 a.m.

Huge round tables were covered with white tablecloths and five-piece settings imported from China, completed with silver flatware and crystal goblets. Daddy's butler, Mani, and the two chauffeurs stood at attention, ready to fulfill their last-minute orders. Mummy had planned for the flowers, the place settings, and the extra hired help. It was a dream come true.

True to the Burmese Buddhist tradition, the bridal chamber was ready, replete with mosquito netting and silver ribbons. Such thought had gone into making this room at our garden house a fit boudoir for a bride.

My luxuries never ended.

Daddy and my sisters came in with gold chains from the jeweler. "It's a wedding tradition," Daddy said. "The corridor leading to the doorway of the bridal chamber must be lined with gold chains. They are only to be removed when the groom pays the required 'ransom' to everyone holding up the golden path as he takes his bride into the chamber."

Preparations completed for the wedding banquet finale to be held that evening, as bride and groom, we changed into the formal Burmese wedding attire—the court dress once worn by royalty and later adopted for Burmese theatre and dance.

And as was the custom, I was adorned with jewelry around my neck, wrists, fingers, and earlobes. My thick, long black hair was divided half into a graceful flowing ponytail and half into a bun adorned with a tiara of a single row of brilliant diamonds—a family heirloom.

Pe walked in, took me in his arms, and whispered. "You look like a beautiful princess. I can't believe you are mine."

"I am. I have always been yours, always."

Promptly at 6 p.m., the dinner gong clanged in a melodious repertoire as the master of ceremonies welcomed everyone.

"I can't believe there are so many guests," I said to Daddy.

"I didn't even expect to see so many people here. Everything looks so beautiful. Nothing is too good for Daddy's little girl."

Course after course was brought by the waiters. Then the five-tiered wedding cake was unveiled. We stood at the bridal table and cut the first piece together, feeding each other our first mouthful. Daddy got up from his seat, teary-eyed, and gave us his blessing. "I'm giving away my daughter, but I have gained a son." He raised his glass to us. "Now, everyone, you are invited to stay for the dancing inside."

Be Still, My Heart

With dinner over, everyone streamed into the house. As the band played, we waltzed our first dance as the guests joined in. Pe whispered into my ear. "Remember when I first met you, my lips were so afraid to say 'I love you'?"

I whispered back. "Remember when, to my surprise, the sudden joy in my heart leapt into your eyes?

Hearts entwined; we each saw only the other. Lost in the wonder of each other and what lay ahead for us, everything else blurred into the distance. Pe had inscribed *Forever Yours, 4th March 1967* on my wedding ring. We belonged to each other forever and ever, from this day forward, never to be separated.

As the band played its last waltz, a scramble was made to the door of the "state" bedroom to block Pe and me from entering. The wedding night ended with the laughing guests lining up and holding gold chains across the bridal chamber door.

"Pay up, Pe! We're not going to let you take Nita in until you give us the ransom money for her!" Amid much laughter, each chain was removed as Pe "paid" them monetary gifts so we could go through—through to a life together, forever.

The Honeymoon

The next day we left for our three-day honeymoon, having rented a bungalow on the white sands of the famous Ngapali beach on the beautiful coast of Burma. We hopped out of the plane and checked in at the beautiful, remote beach resort as husband and wife. Our little bungalow was right on the nearly untouched beachfront of the silver sands, where the deep blue waves lapped the shore with a rhythmic, soothing sound. Coconut groves provided both seclusion and enchantment to the inhabitants of each of the tiny bungalows.

We enjoyed the relaxing days as husband and wife, drinking sweet milk from fresh coconuts. And we swam in the ocean at night, unaware of sharks or jellyfish. We both were so shy and somewhat innocent that, though we were married, we felt guilty sharing a room and sharing a bed.

Aye and Vic had married the same year and had also enjoyed a Ngapali beach honeymoon. But Aye and I never dreamed of the paths that lay ahead for us. Although our lives as physicians' wives became so totally different, we remained closely connected even after several decades of forced separation. As for Pe and me, we had no notion of the upcoming torrential rapids that would threaten to drown us.

Part III
Survival Against All Odds

Chapter 19

A Journey into the Unknown

It's the beauty within us that makes it possible
for us to recognize the beauty around us.
The question is not what you look at but what you see.
–Henry David Thoreau[1]

If you can see all the beauty around you,
you will also see it within.
–Darren Paul Thorn[2]

"...and in the wilderness.
There you saw how the LORD your God carried you,
as a father carries his son,
all the way you went until you reached this place."
–Deuteronomy 1:31 NIV

I would like to say that Pe and I lived happily ever after, but an unseen hand was tightening around us. I would later discover it was a loving cord that drew us to each other and to God Himself. "For richer, for poorer, for better, for worse, in sickness and in health, till death do us part." These vows echoed in my mind as I followed my husband, who, through love exhibited in cherishing and consistent care, would lead me to his loving God.

Our idyllic honeymoon over, Pe was ready to take me back with him to his outpost in the village of Palai, an unknown, untouched, hygiene-deficient village in hot, arid Central Burma. The summons to transfer was by order of the health minister, who was infuriated with my brother-in-law Patrick because he would not consent to the premises of the socialist way of medicine. At least, that was the minister's interpretation. However, Patrick himself was untouchable because he was a national tennis champion who partnered in doubles with the president's wife. So the health minister struck out at Pe, Patrick's closest relative.

At his inquisition, Patrick famously borrowed the line, "You can take a horse to water, but you can't make him drink." The health minister's vendetta was to punish his nemesis's younger brother, who had just graduated from medical school.

Pe was told, "Dr. Pe Than Tin, I am sorry, but it is a government mandate and a requirement. You will need to leave immediately."

"So," Pe responded, "I am to be transplanted to the worst possible area to work at a completely desolate, deficient hospital? I was told that there is no medical outreach in that area. I will be the only physician and surgeon for over one hundred thousand villagers?"

"Precisely. That is why we are sending you there."

Post-Honeymoon Bunk Beds

We were to ride on the train from Rangoon to Mandalay. But because he had been busy, Pe forgot to book our transit early despite my dad's express instructions. So, we purchased our tickets at the station and got the only train out. We hopped on a narrow, ancient train and waved goodbye to our parents and my sisters.

"I'm sorry we didn't get a carriage to ourselves, but it will be okay. We'll make it work."

I looked into the interior of our carriage. "Hmmm. Because of the last-minute tickets, we must sleep on bunk beds on our one-day post-honeymoon night—with a little old lady whose bed is only two feet away from ours?"

We both collapsed on the bottom bunk with laughter as the old lady watched us.

"We need to go to sleep now. We have a long way to go. I'll take the top bunk. Goodnight. I love you."

"Goodnight. I love you too."

Leaning over from the top bunk, Pe smiled. "Hello, Darling, isn't this fun? I miss you."

I smiled up at him, "I miss you too! I want to be where you are. Can you help me climb up?"

We snuggled in the top bunk and fell asleep to the sound of the steady chugging of the train and the distant sounds of the night.

I slept fitfully and did not wake up when the train started slowing down.

"Wake up, Darling." Pe was sitting up, rubbing his eyes, and stifling a yawn. "The train is getting ready to stop. We will get off here at the Mandalay station and catch a bus to Monywa. Our bags are packed and ready to go.

We can just go the way we are. We can brush our teeth when we can get some water." He helped me down.

It felt strange that there was no maid to get my glass of water and a clean towel. Instead, I would have to wait for water just so I could brush my teeth.

My new life had begun.

I Didn't Sign Up for This

Pe helped me up onto the packed open-air bus. "I'm sorry there are no seats, but at least we have some standing room."

"I'll sit on the wheel hump and hold my duffle bag."

Holding the rest of the bags, Pe agreed. "I'll stand close and try to keep you from falling off." I felt safe with my shoulder against his hip.

At a sharp turn, I slid off the wheel hump. He moved in closer. "Darling, will you be all right? It won't be too long, maybe about three hours. We'll stop for a little bit in Monywa and have something to eat."

I smiled at him, "Don't worry, I'm all right. Hopefully, it won't be bumpy like this all the way. What time is it?"

"It's about 7 a.m. We got off the train at 6 a.m., and we'll get to Monywa about 11 a.m. The doctor in Monywa said when we get in, we should come by, freshen up, and have lunch."

"Will we drive to our new house from there?"

Pe chuckled. "From there, we will have to take an open-air truck carrying rice bags and other dry goods. Most of the roads are just dirt, so it will be a bit dusty. There won't be any seats, but the rice bags will be comfortable to sit on, and I brought an umbrella to shield your pretty face from the sun."

Sit on rice bags? No seats? Breathe easy, Nita, Pe's already told you what to expect. You knew it wouldn't be easy. Relax. Breathe gently and long. He whom your soul loves is right beside you. He whom your heart has longed for is with you forever. I fingered my shiny wedding ring. The engraving was printed on my heart. Nothing mattered as long as I was by his side.

"We will cross the Chindwin River on a ferry boat." He looked at me with his tongue in his cheek, "And when we get to a village close to Palai, we will ride on a bullock cart to the hospital and our house."

I looked up at him, trying to balance myself on the wheel hump of the bus. "Will it be a long ride? I have never ridden on a bullock cart."

"It will be bumpy on the roads as most of them are off the beaten tracks. But it will only be for about an hour, and we should be home just before dark."

I beamed at him and nodded. "That will be nice. I can't wait to set up our home. I brought some pretty material to sew curtains for the windows."

My search, which had been evasive yet never far from my mind, had, in fact, begun on a path that was foreign to me. I did not realize I was on the brink of being moved out of my comfort zone into a new normal.

I had no idea I would be squeezed, kneaded, shaped, and molded by the intense hardship entering our lives as my young doctor husband and I were moved to this remote, underdeveloped town in upper Burma. It was there that everything in my life— every luxury that had been my birthright, every necessity that was always at my fingertips, even my safety and all that was formerly predictable—would be stripped away from me.

Chapter 20

Out of My Comfort Zone

Where you go I will go, and where you stay I will stay.
Your people will be my people and your God my God.
–Ruth 1:16 NIV

March 13, 1967; Palai, Gangaw Township, Central Burma

We passed desolate stretches of dusty open spaces. Then, we finally reached a clearing with a few small huts and a bigger hut that looked like an elongated cow shed with roofing that seemed, to my city eyes, like dry grass matted together.

"Why is he stopping the bullock cart? Are we going to get off here?"

We were at the seventh hut, which was made of bamboo, had a tin roof, and was raised on stilts. It seemed to be leaning a little toward the right. Nearby was a smaller hut that looked like the outhouses I had seen in my encyclopedias.

"Here we are, Darling. Welcome to our new home."

He then waved his hand toward the elongated shed. "That building is our hospital. I will show it to you later when you have rested."

He searched my face. He had already warned me of the poverty, disease, and how desolate the place would be.

Shakily, I smiled up at him. "This is our home. All I want is to be with you." We walked up the three rickety steps made of bamboo sticks cut in half and nailed together.

Before he swung open the door, which had no latch, he tenderly lifted my face so I could look into his eyes. There was a look of concern for me, but I noticed a gentleness and a calmness at the same time.

"What helped me when I came here the first time was to stop and pray, thanking God for providing this home. I ask Him every morning to bless this home, where you and I will begin our life together."

He stopped, took me in his arms, and bowed his head. "Dear Lord, bless our lives together here. Make Yourself known in this hard place. Help me to minister to the people here and to wisely and generously use the gifts You have given me. I pray that this will be our sanctuary and that You will keep us safe here and provide for us. In Jesus's name, Amen."

Tears brimmed from my eyes, and I wiped them away on his shirt sleeve.

The house was a single room divided by a bamboo mat nailed to some old wood to provide a partition. One half was our bedroom, which was the width and breadth of a king-size bed. The other half was our kitchen, where a kerosene stove sat on a small shelf, leaving just enough space for a crude wooden dining table and two small, uncomfortable straight chairs.

I smiled bravely. "We'll make it cozy, Darling. The drapes I brought will hang nicely on this little kitchen window."

He put our bags in the corner beside our bed. He chuckled, "You won't need to unpack because we have no closets or chest of drawers."

He had previously told me there was no electricity, no running water, and no grocery stores. There was just a clustering of small huts and a village well that ran dry, giving out only a trickle of drinking and bathing water. But this was more desolate than I had imagined.

The First Day

Looking back on my first day there, I can now laugh, but I wasn't laughing then. Pe had gone to work, and when he came home that evening, he found me crying. "What's happened, Darling? This is our first day at our together home."

I could not stop the tears. "You left this morning for work, and you didn't kiss me goodbye."

He caressed my hair and kissed me on the forehead, "Oh, Sweetheart, I am so sorry. You were sleeping so peacefully I didn't want to wake you up. I look after all the villagers of this township, so I have to leave when the sun comes up. I only have one health assistant that the World Health Organization has given me, and he always takes off all day on the UNICEF motorbike to go to the surrounding areas."

I stifled my tears and kissed him back. "I love you. I know they all need you. It's just that it was a long day, and I was so lonely."

He held me close and thanked me for coming out to be with him. "It was very lonely for me, too, when I was by myself, Darling. The work here is difficult with the few instruments they have given me. There are very few supplies and so many sick people. There is no other doctor for miles around. But the thought of seeing your sweet face gets me through the day."

I hugged him close and pulled his head down so he could rest on my shoulder. I felt his tiredness. I loved him more than I had before. I honored him more than I had before. "Dear Heart, dedicated and giving, even when you're exhausted. You're mustering up unimaginable courage to go to that hut and give these villagers a fighting chance." I kissed his weary forehead.

He took my hand and prayed before our first meal in our own home. I loved hearing him thank his heavenly Father, and I wished I knew how.

As we sat close together, my husband's gentle voice came close to my ear, "I missed you all day, Darling. How did it go for you?"

I was ready to chat. "Oh, I sewed the curtains for the windows. I wish I could have had my sewing machine, but I did it by hand. Do you like them? It does make this home look cozy and pretty." I chattered on. With no telephone, there had been no one to talk to. "You know, it was so funny this afternoon. While I was cooking our dinner on the stove, about fifteen villagers just stood outside, staring at me and not saying anything. And then, when I went to get water from that stone jar outside, they followed me."

He murmured something and was almost asleep, still sitting up on our hard dining chair.

"Sweetheart, you must be exhausted! I put your Bible beside your bed on a little block of wood I found outside. I can read it to you if you'd like."

He smiled and nodded.

My Rock and My Fortress

We lay down on the hard mattress. I read a passage Pe had marked, and then I massaged his stiff neck and back. He fell asleep almost immediately, but I kept on reading. The page was highlighted in yellow, and he had written a few notes in the margin. *You are my Rock and my Fortress, my God in whom I trust.* I wondered what that meant. I made a mental note to ask him the next day.

His Bible was well-worn. He must have had it since he was a teenager. He had told me that ever since he was a little boy, his parents had taken him with them to Sunday School and church. He said he liked listening to the sermons, but he loved reading the Bible for himself because he found hidden treasures in it. His parents were good Christians, and after his mother died, he continued attending church with his dad.

Yet beyond that, something about him seemed almost otherworldly, as if he was actually with Jesus all the time.

I closed his Bible and reached to put it on the little wooden box beside our bed, and our wedding program fell out. I had not noticed it before, but a Bible verse was printed on the back. "Where you go, I will go, and where you stay, I will stay. Your people will be my people and your God my God" (Ruth 1:16 NIV). I thought about that verse. That would be so true for me. I wished, however, that his God would be my God too.

Chapter 21

Am I Up for the Challenge?

Embrace each challenge in your life as opportunity for self-transformation.
–Bernie Siegel[1]

For our light and momentary troubles are achieving for us
an eternal glory that far outweighs them all.
So we fix our eyes not on what is seen, but on what is unseen,
since what is seen is temporary, but what is unseen is eternal.
–2 Corinthians 4:17–18 NIV

Two weeks later, I was excited with my new find. "I found a muddy river several miles away. I learned to wash clothes by beating them on a rock. Isn't that awesome?"

Pe smiled, "Your brilliant little brain is always working overtime. I knew you would improvise."

I carried water in a pail and walked a half mile each trip so we could have some bathing and cooking water, which I poured into a rusty container behind our shack. With no bathroom, this was where I had to bathe, almost fully clothed and in full view of the curious villagers. That was awkward. When Pe came home, I asked him, "Maybe one of the men could rig up a bamboo partition outside the wall of the hut. What do you think?"

"Of course, Darling. I'll ask one of the patients. They have no money to pay for my treatment and are always asking if they could do something for us."

I tried to make life as good as I could with what little we had. And he would say, "Thank you, Darling. You make everything seem beautiful, and you never complain about roughing it with me in this village. Soon we will be able to have a better life. You deserve so much."

I was glad that I could make it bearable for him as well. Looking at his gentle face made it all so worthwhile "I'm so happy that we are together. That's all that matters. You know I would go anywhere with you."

And he would say, "You amaze me, my little princess. For having had everyone at home taking care of you, you have turned out to be a little trooper."

The heat in central Burma was scorching. We had no refrigeration, air conditioning, or even electric fans in a climate where the temperature would climb to 115 degrees. Having never been in the kitchen at my parent's house, I now learned to painstakingly dry meat and preserve vegetables after "shopping" at our once-a-week market day stall. I'd pick up some stringy-looking beef, and the villagers would sometimes bring small chickens into the little coop they had made for us.

On market day, woven bamboo baskets on the ground contained a few vegetables—mostly corn, some dark green leaves, potatoes, and nuts still in their shells. I dutifully filled up my basket. Some days there was no meat. The live chickens in the coops were scrawny, and I had no way of preparing them. I never needed to get cooking oil or rice because, in gratitude for Pe's services, the patients would come by and pour oil into our huge stone pots and rice into the metal bins outside our door.

Pe was always considerate and kind. He tried to make life as tolerable as possible for me, but he was kept busy with patients at all hours.

"I don't have anyone to assist me except for the compounder who takes care of the medicines and drugs I need for the patients. His niece serves as the hospital secretary and holds the flashlight for me when I must do emergency surgery in the dark."

Though he was working around the clock, he felt a deep satisfaction knowing he could save some of the people from premature death, which was prevalent in such a village that lacked hygiene and had few medical resources.

Dry Heat and Wet Towels

Our little shack was a challenge. As torrential rain or oppressive heat beat down mercilessly through the gaping tin roof and ill-fitting slats that were the walls of our one-room hut, I relentlessly moved our furniture around, trying to prevent it from getting wet. Still, one day an unexpected storm broke loose and completely soaked our mattress. In sheer desperation, I sat on the bed and cried.

When Pe came home, his eyes took in the chaos, including the soaked towels and askew mattress. He held me close and caressed my tousled hair.

I was able to giggle. "Well, at least this awful heat and my towels quickly soaked up the huge wet spots in the mattress and kept the wooden floor-boards dry."

Intruders

A single shaky door, which could not be locked or keep out unwanted visitors, led to the hospital compound. The only window, located above the tiny kerosene camping stove that sat on the kitchen floor, looked out to our outhouse several yards away.

Pe came home from the hospital late one day and found me crouched behind the bed's headboard in the dimness of the shack's interior. "What happened, my Darling? Why are you shaking?" He pulled me to him and held me close until my sobs subsided.

"Two men came through the door, and they were drunk. So I went to hide." I shuddered. "They stopped at the water pot, got a drink, and then left noisily. I was so scared."

He soothed, "Of course you were. I am so glad they didn't see you. Next time we can get to Monywa, we will buy a door latch."

To a girl who had taken everything for granted, every day here was a challenge. I shed lots of tears but also had lots of laughter and endless love.

In for a Shock

My parents decided to come out to see us. They wanted to see the place that was our home, and Daddy had his chauffeur drive them all the way to Palai with a night stop each in Sagaing and Monywa. Crossing the Chindwin River was a challenge, but the car and its passengers all arrived safely after traveling three days on the dirt roads.

"Hey Tita, why are you living so far out here?" thirteen-year-old Chicky chirped.

Esme shrugged her shoulders, "I can't believe you have been living in this awful place for three months already. I'd come back while I have the chance if I were you."

Gail just shook her head. She looked inside the shack and saw the stark bareness and the poverty. She looked at my face. Perhaps she saw my happiness, and her face softened.

The village well gave a trickling of muddy water that I boiled for hot tea, but the weather was scorching and humid, and flies swarmed around the food.

I think Daddy and Mummy were shocked, to say the least, but they didn't say anything. I guess they knew my life was now with Pe. They trusted him and knew he would take care of me.

Pe hurried back from the hospital, and they all hugged him. He saw that Daddy was uncomfortable in the sweltering heat, so he took some water and spread it around the chair Daddy was sitting in.

They were thankful that they were able to see us, but because there were no hotels or any place to stay the night, they drove back the same day, leaving in the early afternoon to get to Monywa before dark.

That night as we cuddled in bed in our one-room, leaky shack, Pe said, "I am so glad you didn't want to go back with your family to Rangoon."

I put his tired head in the crook of my neck and whispered, "You are my family now."

The verse Pe read that night made me happy when he explained it. He said our hardship here was just temporary, and God had eternal things prepared for those who love Him that we are not yet able to see. He said it would all be wonderful, and we could not imagine the things we have never heard, seen, or conceived of that would be ours.

I wondered what those things were, but just thinking about them made my hard life here in this village bearable.

Chapter 22

A Cobra, a Waltz Under the Silver Moon, and a Sand Oven

Life takes us to unexpected places
Love takes us home
–Melissa McClone[1]

I had somewhat learned to tolerate the thought of scorpions falling out from tree branches, but when Pe warned me of other dangers, I became very cautious of my surroundings.

"Be careful when you go outside, Darling. Vipers and cobras crawl and lurk in the undergrowth, looking for their prey. They also find places under the house to hibernate."

One incident stands forever stamped on my memory. Pe had hopped out from the low kitchen window, as he often did out of fun and convenience, to go to the outhouse twenty yards away. As I watched him jump down, my eyes widened, and my heart skipped a beat. In that split second, I saw a cobra raise its head near him, its long neck and body quivering and slithering upwards, ready to strike.

With a quick reflex, Pe pointed to an old golf club in the corner of the room next to the window that was our only weapon. "Quick, pass me that stick!"

I grabbed it and passed it on to him. I closed my eyes, not daring to look at what was happening.

I heard a sharp *thwack* as the iron hit the serpent's head with such force that it died on impact. Trembling, I could not hold back my tears of fear and relief as Pe clambered back through the window to hold me in a quick embrace.

"It's okay, Darling, it is dead."

As I watched Pe open the door and walk along the narrow path, my heart was still pounding, but I was so grateful that his quick thinking had taken care of the snake. What would I have done if the cobra had struck him? I didn't want to dwell on what might have been.

Treasure These Moments

Pe came bounding into the hut one day, his eyes sparkling. "We have some free time. Let's go on an adventure. The compounder said we could borrow his bicycle. I want to take you on the six-mile ride to the off-the-trail hot springs I told you about."

Such moments when the health assistant returned early from his trips, allowing us to slip away, were rare. We treasured those times we could just be young marrieds.

He pedaled down the beaten path while I sat behind, holding on to his narrow waist and leaning on his muscled back. We arrived at the clearing and waded, fully clothed, into the hot springs, which flowed in as a small waterfall. We brought soap and shampoo, and Pe washed my thick black hair, which had grown down beyond my waist, and he braided it into two pigtails so it wouldn't get tangled. The hot sun on our backs would dry our clothes and hair on the way back.

"This is sheer delight," I said. "I wish we could come here every day."

He held me close. "Treasure these moments, Darling. It is ours for right now."

Moonlit nights were also a joy; though these trips were rare, each was precious. Especially dear to me was when the water was rhythmically hitting the smooth rocks, and we were ankle-deep in the warm water. Pe held me close as he hummed the tune of "Unchained Melody," and we waltzed to the soothing sounds. In those moments, nothing mattered except our love for each other. Time stood still as we swayed tenderly under the silver moon.

A Sand Oven

I woke up with a start one morning, realizing Pe had already left for the hospital. I looked at the little wall calendar with its happy little flower sketches. April 16, 1967. The seventh anniversary of the day we fell in love—I wanted to make it special. I also wanted to keep it a secret from Pe.

When a village boy passed by our house, I ran outside to stop him. "Ko Khin, here is some money. Will you see if you can buy a chicken for me from the weekly market and clean it for me?"

He brought back a small chicken, and I roasted it in a makeshift oven by putting sand in an empty powdered milk tin given by UNICEF for our village babies. I seasoned the chicken and placed it in the tin on the kerosene stove so it could cook slowly, adding potatoes and a bit of straggly green beans to make up the meal. I had also saved some eggs, so I whipped them with a small amount of sugar and the can of milk I had brought from Mummy's kitchen to make a beautiful flan for dessert.

After a life of extravagant wealth, to be happy in my present existence attests to the power of love and a life of purpose.

Till Death Do Us Part

That evening I whisked Pe from the door into our bedroom half of the hut. He sensed my excitement. "What have you got up your little sleeve, Darling? You look like you are going to burst." I had laid out his white silk jacket and black silk trousers, complete with a red bow tie, gold cufflinks, and shiny patent leather shoes. "Wash up and put these on, Darling. I brought them in the bag I was holding on our trip out here. It was the bag I wouldn't let you carry for me."

He laughed as he carried me up in his strong arms. "Happy Anniversary, my sweet little wife. I'm sorry I can't get flowers for you, but you have my heart."

We dressed up as though we were going to a fancy restaurant. Then, hand in hand, we walked to the kitchen table, which I had decorated with a candle, a lace tablecloth, and pretty napkins.

I took out the two pretty plates I had hidden behind our everyday ones and heaped the roasted chicken, potatoes, and string beans on them. Pe grasped my hand as he gave thanks to his God for all He had provided.

The love in his eyes was all I needed and made the hardship bearable as we sat in quiet companionship, enjoying our simple meal.

Once we got into bed, Pe read from his Bible, as he always did. "This is called The Love Chapter. This is what the pastor read at our wedding." His voice was soothing, and the words were beautiful.

When he finished, we read our marriage vows from the program tucked in his Bible: "For better, for worse, for richer, for poorer, in sickness and in health, to love and to cherish, till death do us part." He continued, "According to God's holy ordinance; and thereto I pledge thee my faith." He took both my hands, looked deep into my eyes, and said, "I have prayed for you every day, that you will come to know my Savior too."

He cradled me in his arms as I went to sleep, feeling safe. I felt such a sense of oneness. A knowledge of belonging. A premonition that something was happening deep in my soul.

Chapter 23

Off the Beaten Path

I have one final word for Christians who serve in this field.
God has placed you right where you are to best glorify Him.
You know the Great Physician and you are His healing hands.
–Russell Gehrlein[1]

Stories of an off-the-beaten-path township physician and surgeon are too numerous to mention here. Pe treated everything from delivering babies on mats on the floor in an unhygienic, outdated hospital to removing tonsils or scraping pterygiums from the corneas of so many eyes.

Once, I walked over to the hospital as it was getting dark, and what I saw gave me the shivers. Pe was sewing up the scalp of a woman's head without any anesthesia or sedative as she knelt on the mud floor outside the hospital. Her husband had axed her and run off.

Pe was using both hands to cauterize and stop the bleeding from the gaping wound.

"Saya, my head hurts, and I can't see. The blood is flowing down my face."

I took a piece of gauze from his makeshift table and wiped the blood. She looked at me with grateful, humble eyes, yet there was a sadness deep within those dull and faded windows of her soul.

I held her hand and told her, "Be brave. You will feel better soon."

My heart hurt for her—not just for the wound or that she had been axed by her husband, but for that broken spirit. In this culture, the man was supreme. *How many times has this happened?* I wondered.

Mya Thit, the compounder, hurried out from the doorway. His voice was concerned, "I don't have the supplies you need, Saya. The shipment is delayed again, and the supplies are very low. There are no Red Cross vehicles available to bring it from Rangoon."

My heart broke. This village hospital needed outside help badly. The entire village had no electricity or running water, Pe had no nurses or other medical staff to assist him, and now he was running out of supplies.

As Pe sutured together the gaping wound on the woman's head, which still bled profusely and ran down her face, the secretary who held the flashlight for him got dizzy, and the flashlight was no longer steady. "Saya, I am going to faint."

I took the flashlight from her. "Don't worry, Tin San Myint. I can take over."

I made her lie down and held the smelling salts to her nose with one hand while I held the flashlight with the other.

"Hold the flashlight steady, Darling. You can leave the smelling salts under her nose. I am going to need help. This lady is not staying still."

I watched Pe's skillful hands while I spoke to the bleeding woman in soothing tones, hoping to calm her hysterical sobs. He put in the last stitches, and as he was cleaning her wound and taping a layer of gauze over it, we heard an agitated voice.

"Saya, please come. This boy has been bitten by a poisonous snake. I think he is near death." A man came in, carrying the still form of a young boy.

Pe laid him on a palette and tried to resuscitate the little boy, who had been bitten in the head by a viper while he was asleep in a monastery. Pe searched for his pulse and took his vitals, but the lifeless boy did not respond.

"It is too late for the anti-venom injections because the venom has reached his brain. I will try to treat him as best I can. The snake must have been biting him on the head all night because there are more than a dozen snake bites on his scalp. I am so sorry, sir."

The little monk was delirious and did not last through the night. He did not seem to have a mother or father accompanying him and must have been given to the monkhood at an early age.

Performing surgeries of every sort, treating malaria and TB patients, and teaching villagers to drink sanitary water and dig outhouses to provide for sanitation were all part of the responsibilities of a rural township medical doctor, and my conscientious husband worked 24 hours a day, seven days a week, leaving very little time to look after himself or invest in our new marriage.

A Divine Source

"I wish I had more time to spend with you," Pe said. "But I cannot leave these people to die without the medical help they need."

"I will help you in any way I can," I replied. "I want to walk beside you."

As we washed up in the bucket of water outside our hut, he looked at me with such love in his kind eyes. "You stand beside me all the time. It brings me such comfort. I am so glad I have you."

We were both tired, and he fell asleep without the nightly reading of his Bible, but he whispered a prayer for his patients just before his thick black lashes closed over his slim cheeks.

I planted a light kiss on his forehead and watched his chest rise and fall with his slow and steady breathing. He was totally relaxed, deep in sleep; his lips curved in a sweet smile as though dreaming of joys unknown.

As I thought about and processed all the work Pe was doing, a feeling rose within me that I could assist him. Perhaps I would be a good helper. In my young life, I was shielded from so much. But this was the real world.

I now saw pain and death and healing. I saw fear and hope and gratitude. I saw my husband as a physician and surgeon who gave himself to heal others. But most of all, I saw Pe as a healer who totally depended on his heavenly Father.

Pe never pushed his faith on me. But he lived it daily and took every opportunity to share God's Word with me. He would tell me that God loved me and that I could trust God just as he did. Yet, he knew it had to be my own decision to come directly to God, confess my need for Jesus as my Savior, and receive His free gift of salvation.

Chapter 24

Survival Against All Odds

*Trouble is an exerciser sent us by a Wisdom wiser than the
mind of man possesses. Doubts and dangers and distresses come
not purposely to best us, but to strengthen and test us.*
–Edgar Albert Guest[1]

*We are hard pressed on every side, but not crushed;
perplexed, but not in despair;
persecuted, but not abandoned;
struck down, but not destroyed.*
–2 Corinthians 4:8–9 NIV

It was now June of our first year at the outpost. The heat was at its
zenith. I was pregnant with our first child, but my pregnancy was
almost cut short as I bounced up and down on bullock carts, our
only means of transport between villages. Finally, after being jarred
and thrown against the roof of a UNICEF jeep as I traveled back
from a week's stay at the home of my brother-in-law Patrick and his
family in Chauk, a region rich in oil and cultivated by the British who
had developed the area, I returned home, not knowing I was bleeding
internally.

I did not want to bother Patrick, so he let me out in front of the hut and did not come in. I climbed up the short, dilapidated steps, pushed open the flimsy wood door to our one-bedroom shack, which, today, strangely enough seemed to welcome me, and I lay down on the bed in a half stupor.

I felt dizzy and could hardly lift my head from my lumpy pillow. Without realizing it, I drifted into unconsciousness as the room darkened. I normally would have lit the kerosene lamps long before Pe came home.

Nightfall came, and darkness enveloped me. I lay there, unaware of what was going on. I didn't know that the shack had slowly turned pitch dark or that I had been bleeding for hours without any medical attention.

I didn't hear Pe call out from the yard, "Darling, I'm home. I am sorry I am so late."

I didn't hear his worried "Oh, my Darling!" as he opened the door and found me bleeding and unresponsive.

I didn't hear him repeating, "Darling, wake up! Speak to me!" when he found me unconscious.

I didn't know he ran back to his cowshed hospital, bringing back the necessary but sparse supplies to resuscitate me and give me immediate medical care.

I didn't know until he told me later that he returned home from a long day at the hospital, excited to see me because I had been away a whole week and was alarmed when he saw me lying on our bed.

As I came to, I saw so much concern and love in Pe's eyes as he held me tight and cradled my head. "I love you so much, Darling. I couldn't bear to lose you."

He made sure I was comfortable for the night, and as he held me, his prayers were the last thing I heard before I went to sleep.

Before he left for work early the next morning, Pe ordered complete bed rest. "We have to make sure you stay well and strong and that our baby will arrive safely."

I nodded weakly. And after he left, I silently cried into my pillow. *Would our baby live?*

Anxious, Alone, and Depressed

I spent the last five months of my pregnancy on the thin mattress in that tin roof shack, which felt hotter than an oven.

Pe could spend very little time with me, although he wanted to be at my side. "I wish I didn't have to leave you by yourself. I will try to come home earlier."

However, some nights were spent crying myself to sleep as my young husband toiled in the hospital shack across the compound, taking care of the sick almost singlehandedly for a township of now close to more than one hundred thousand people.

During those long, hot, uncomfortable days, as I lay in bed under that tin roof, I longed for my mother and three sisters to hold my hand, talk to me, and comfort me. There were no telephones, so we had no communication except for letters and cards that took three or four weeks to arrive.

Hot, pregnant, and depressed, I often wished I were back home, where life was beautiful but now only a dream in my exhausted and chaotic mind. Yet whenever Pe returned, our little shack once more became a haven as love overcame and brought me back to my chosen life, where just being with my husband was what mattered.

Did I really want to go back to the life I had known, where I was rich and pampered and had searched for meaning for so long? Here in this little hut, in this back-of-beyond place with my soulmate by my side, something beautiful was slowly being created in my soul, even as a little being was being formed within me. No, I couldn't imagine going back.

Yet, one day as Pe came home from the hospital and we were preparing to have dinner, I had something scary to tell him.

"You know that tree a few feet from our hut? Well, I have been taking a bamboo mat and trying to take a rest under its shade when it gets unbearable in here. Guess what happened today?"

He laughed as he put his hands beside my now-swollen face, looking deeply into my eyes, which still had a glint of fear. "A scorpion fell from one of the branches onto your mat, and I'm sure he wanted to get away from you!"

"How did you know?" I was now giggling. "Of course, I got away from him too."

Just Stand Still, the Lord Will Protect Us

In my seventh month of pregnancy, we had tornado-strength high winds and unrelenting monsoon rain. This caused a flood that forced our house, my bamboo matted make-shift kitchen, and our outhouse to float into the fields, causing unsanitary conditions as water from seepage bubbled up through our slatted floors.

Pe came rushing in as the flimsy walls and the roof of the hospital were swept away. "Quick, Darling, we have to get up on the dining table. The waters are not safe."

He helped my now-heavy form onto the solid wooden table, which was still intact. My meager stock of onions and shriveled potatoes were on the table, and he made room for my swollen legs to have a firm foothold before he climbed up on the table to hold me steady.

As we stood, watching the now-rising seepage water rushing through the floorboards, I pointed and let out a scream. "Look!" Rattlesnakes and slimy water snakes slithered by in the rushing rivers.

"I know. That is why it is not safe to get off the table." Pe stood alert, holding high a machete to protect his shaken and frightened wife and the mother of his unborn child.

I was trembling, and my knees were knocking. I wanted to sit down, but the water was almost reaching to the tops of the table legs.

Just then, a strong gust of wind blew the tin roof completely off our hut and carried it away. As he held me close, Pe said quietly, "Don't be scared. Just stay still. I have asked the Lord to protect us." He began to quote from memory: "He who dwells in the shelter of the Most High will abide under the shadow of the Almighty. I will say of the Lord, my refuge and my fortress, my God, in whom I trust."

He looked intently into my eyes. "The Lord will protect. He will provide. And His presence will be with us. He has promised in Psalm 91, so don't be afraid."

I was still shaking, but his voice calmed me. He was so confident in whom he believed.

With the roof gone from our one-room house, we could see swaying coconut trees nearby where several men had shimmied up to get away from the roaring torrent of the sweeping floods.

"Do you think they all drowned? How terrible. I hope they will all be safe."

Finally, the floods abated, leaving mud, debris, and remnants that had floated from our kitchen and outhouse.

In time, the flimsy roof was fixed, and the rough wooden floor with the big gaping slats was cleaned. Our outhouse and our lean-to kitchen were rebuilt and became usable again. Together, we had made it through yet another storm.

Hard Trip to Rangoon

As the birth of our first baby drew near, we made plans to return to Rangoon so the delivery would occur in a city hospital.

"We need our baby to have a fighting chance to live. I've seen so many babies here struggle through to term, but in these unsanitary conditions, many do not live after birth."

We spent nights talking about who our baby would look like. "If the baby is a little girl, I know she will look just like you. Maybe she'll burst into the scene with little pigtails and a pink ribbon," Pe whispered as we sat together on our bed, holding each other.

"I know our baby will look like you," I whispered back. "He has to be an angelic little boy."

Soon it was time, and we started off on our journey to have our baby at Rangoon General Hospital.

What seemed hilarious afterward but was scary at the time was that an hour after we left Palai, the weather turned for the worse. Black clouds gathered and looked ominous. We had been dropped off by a bullock cart and walked down the dusty path to the jetty at the Chindwin River, where we would cross over to Monywa, take a bus to Mandalay, and then a train to Rangoon.

We got to the jetty, but the boat tied up at the dock was not the one we were taking to get across.

"Wait here, Darling. I will go down the bank to see if there is a passenger boat coming that will take us to the other side."

As Pe walked away, strong gusts of wind whipped the swaying coconut trees, and the sky continued to darken. Suddenly, tornado-like winds began sweeping through, causing roosters and chickens and baskets of produce to be pulled into the whirlwind and swirled up into the air.

Two men from the docked boat saw me holding my swollen belly. "Ah Mar Gyi, come with us. We will help you onto the boat to shelter from the storm."

When Pe returned to where I had been standing and saw that I wasn't at the jetty, he became worried. "Where are you, Darling?" he shouted at the top of his voice. "I can't see you."

I tried to get his attention, but he was standing transfixed as he stared up at the sky. Later, I found out he thought I had been caught up in the whirlwind of dust and heavy debris. Finally, soaked to the skin from the sudden downpour and frantic for my safety, Pe hurried to the dock, straight to the ferryboat I was in to see if he could get help to locate me.

Waving my white scarf, I screamed at the top of my voice above the howling winds and the dashing waves. "I'm here! I'm in the boat! Get inside. Quickly!" A jagged streak of lightning flashed, and the roar of thunder followed. The men opened the door and pulled Pe inside.

I will never forget the look on my husband's face and the way he held me close when he discovered I was safe. "I thought you had been blown away."

The storm abated as quickly as it had arrived, and we were finally able to get onto the passenger boat waiting for us farther downstream. Then, after crossing the Chindwin River to Monywa, we managed to get on a truck going to Mandalay, where we got tickets for the last train.

Pe was carrying our suitcase and my night bag as we approached the train when I abruptly, not seeing the high platform, fell face down on the hard, dirty stone pavement.

"A Ma, A Ma, are you alright?" Two well-meaning women ran over to massage my swollen belly thinking it would ease the pain, but Pe got to me in time.

"Thank you, A Daw Gyi. I am a doctor."

He bowed to them and smiled, then picked me up from the pavement. "Breathe, Darling. I will get you to the hospital as soon as we get to Rangoon. Let's get on this train, and I will check your pulse and listen for the baby." He helped me up on the train and tenderly placed me in a corner seat, rolling up his jacket to put behind my head. "Keep on breathing gently. I will take care of you."

Pe sterilized and bandaged the small wound on my cheek. He checked my pulse and, with his stethoscope, listened to my heartbeat, then that of the baby. He nodded. "You and the baby are going to be all right."

Pe kept a close watch on me, checking my vitals—making sure I was okay. It had been exhausting for him to take this long trip straight from work, but his head was bowed in prayer as I leaned on his shoulder just before I closed my tired eyes. I heard him breathe a sigh of relief. "Thank you, Jesus, for taking care of my sweetheart. Protect our little boy."

He cradled my head as I dozed off and slept through the entire eight-hour train ride.

Chapter 25

The Room with Twelve Beds and a Candy-Striped Nurse

For you created my inmost being;
you knit me together in my mother's womb.
I praise you because I am fearfully and wonderfully made.
–Psalm 139:13–14a NIV

But then the Candy Striper would appear with that candy cane dress
so brightly and cheerful, yet it was the smile, the calm hello,
that lifted suffering hearts from their stress. One touch of care meant so much,
for they would hold your hand, truly wanting to know who you were.
–Harry William Robbins[1]

Rangoon, December 11, 1967

We got to Rangoon late the next morning and checked in at Rangoon General Hospital, now run by the socialist state.

"My wife would like a private room, please. She is Dr. Daw Khin May's patient." Pe smiled at the hospital receptionist.

"The registration shows that Daw Nita is in a room with eleven other women."

"May she have a private room, please? I used to work at this hospital, and patients were always given a private room if they could pay for it."

"Did you hear what I said? Daw Nita is registered in a room with eleven other patients. This privilege has been given only because she is a doctor's wife."

There were women screaming on mats on the floor of the corridors.

"Could she have a private nurse?"

"There are no private nurses available."

"May I please speak to the supervisor?"

The supervisor was called in. She knew our parents and had worked with Pe when he interned at the hospital. She looked away, "I am sorry, Dr. Pe Than Tin, but this room is all we have, and the circulating nurses will take care of her. We will make sure you are called when it is time."

Socialism was making its mark.

It was my first pregnancy, and although I was already in pain, hours went by with nothing happening. I made several trips up and down the corridor, navigating past the gurney beds that lined the hall and trying to ignore the moaning that poured from various rooms. Then, I would return to the room with the twelve beds and fragmented medical care.

Thankfully, my sister Gail arrived and was permitted to come into the room. "Let me walk you down the hall to the bathroom. A warm shower will help you."

Afterward, she said, "I'm sorry you couldn't get a private room or nurse. Things have changed so much." Indeed, socialism was making its mark.

I nodded. "The water was soothing. That was a good idea."

We walked together for several minutes before we went back to my bed.

Gail whispered, "I guess that after working all those hours for so many months, Pe is finally able to catch up with his sleep. He found a corner just outside the corridor, and we put three chairs in a row. When I went to check on him, he was sound asleep."

"I think we should let him sleep. He has been exhausted. He has been taking care of me and is still very tired from our long trip and the never-ending responsibilities at the hospital in Palai."

When visiting hours at the hospital ended, Gail kissed my forehead and said, "I've got to leave now. Try to sleep, Nita. I will be back tomorrow."

Hours passed. No one came to check on me. My doctor had not come to see me, and the nurses were busy taking care of so many pregnant women. I wished I could hold Pe's hand.

You're Taking Up Space

I tried to sleep, but all night long, contractions came in rapid succession, and I almost passed out. A nurse was passing by and, seeing that I was in pain, recognized my labor was progressing and took me to the delivery room. But within seconds, she turned around and wheeled me right back to the room with the twelve beds.

"We can't let you take up the space in the crowded delivery room. You'll have to wait until you are ready to deliver."

After four hours with no nurse to help me, I walked to the lavatory down the hall. Within minutes I felt sharp pains and flagged a candy-striped nurse in training. "Please help me. I think I am going to have my baby."

My son's head was already presenting itself with his shock of black hair visible, and she quickly put me in a wheelchair and got me a bed in the delivery room.

"I'll try and get you help right away." She patted my hand and smoothed my brow, furrowed with pain. They could not reach my doctor, who was the attending physician and a friend of the family, so the resident physician delivered my baby. Pe was not allowed in.

"Your son was blue at birth, and his breathing was labored because of the pethidine we injected before he was delivered. You were in so much pain. He is being given oxygen right now."

It was some time before I could hold him, but he was a beautiful baby. He was our own, and I held him close.

"Oh, my sweet baby, your Phay Phay and I love you so much and have been waiting for you. I don't know how we can take you back to Palai." My tears fell on his cheek, and I wiped them away as I looked up and saw Pe hurrying toward us.

He had been allowed into the room with the twelve beds where I lay nursing my baby. He knelt beside us and gathered us both in his strong arms, kissing our foreheads. "I love you, Sweetheart. I love you, my son. Let's call him Zaw. He fought through a near miscarriage and a difficult birth. He is full of courage. Thank You, Lord, that You kept them both safe."

I knew Pe had to return to our outpost after seeing our son. He bent down and held me close to him. "I am so sad that I must leave right now and return to our outpost when you need me so much. I need you too, Darling, and our baby needs both of us, but I must go back."

I pressed my tear-stained face into his shoulder. "I will miss you so much, but your God will take care of all of us while we are apart."

"Yes, He will. He always has. I will surround you both with my prayers. Come home soon, Darling. I will count the days until I see you and little Zaw."

My parents were concerned about the unhygienic conditions in Palai—that I would take Zaw back too early. But Pe agreed I should stay in Rangoon with my parents until Zaw was six months old.

I missed Pe every day. I missed his wise words, his calming influence, and most of all, his quiet faith that always kept me going.

Chapter 26

Mashed Potatoes and Bible Stories

Life is not always a matter of holding good cards,
but sometimes, playing a hand well
–Jack London[1]

I have learned to be content whatever the circumstances.
I know what it is to be in need, and I know what it is to have plenty.
I have learned the secret of being content in any and every situation,
whether well fed or hungry, whether living in plenty or in want.
I can do all this through him who gives me strength.
–Philippians 4:11b–13 NIV

After being cooped up in a steaming hot, one-room shack for almost a year, it was sheer luxury to bask on satin sheets tucked into a king-size four-poster bed in a spacious air-conditioned bedroom with an attached bathroom. The windows overlooking green lawns, colorful flower beds, and vistas of well-appointed surroundings, complete with maids and butlers, felt nothing short of extravagant.

It was strange for me not to get up at the crack of dawn to pull water from the well and get the kettle boiling so we could have sterilized drinking water. Stranger still to have one of the maids bring me thin slices of perfectly toasted bread slathered with honey and a steaming cup of coffee.

Luxurious as it was, I longed to be with Pe. Six months dragged slowly by, but soon it was time to go home to Palai. Zaw had grown into a beautiful six-month-old infant. He was a happy and healthy boy, well-loved by his grandparents and aunts. With a sanitary environment and the medical care he needed, those months in Rangoon had been critical before we traveled to Palai.

Daddy made the arrangements for our trip back. He called his cousin. "Hi Ernest, when is your next flight to Mandalay? Nita and the baby need to get back to Palai, and it would be so helpful if you could take them with you. Pe will be there to meet them."

"I'll fly them up in my private plane to Mandalay, and he can meet us at the airport and take them home."

"Thanks, old chap. I appreciate your offer."

There were no telephone lines to Palai, so Daddy wired the nearest outpost of our arrival date in Mandalay. Pe and I were excited that we would finally see each other again.

We touched down at the Mandalay airport, where my husband was already waiting for us. "Thank you, Uncle Ernest. We couldn't have made it here without you."

"Any time."

In moments, Pe and I were in each other's arms. "I missed you so much," I cried into his broad shoulder.

"I have missed you more. The nights have been so long without you. I have pictured your sweet face and bright eyes watching out for me each evening, having dinner ready for me in our cozy little house."

He held us out at arm's length and kissed our son's cheeks as Zaw smiled and cooed at his Phay Phay. I watched with tears in my eyes as he held our son up in the air and then brought him back into the cradle of his arms. As we left the gate, Pe huddled us close to him and thanked God for giving us a safe trip. My heart could not contain itself.

The long journey back home was tiring, and as we rode the bullock cart home, I sighed with relief and exhaustion. Seeing my husband holding our son was like a balm to my tired spirit.

Not Just to Survive but to Thrive

Keeping a home for the three of us was very different than keeping a home for two. We were still like newlyweds, but now we had a baby to care for. I was grateful when one of the young lads came to help me by bringing several buckets from the well and pouring them into a stone jar a few yards from our house so I could wash the baby's nappies and our clothes.

In between, I was cooking all our meals on the small kerosene camp stove. And when I did, I had no place to put Zaw down where I could trust he wouldn't crawl away and get hurt. Besides the noticeably perilous surroundings, there were still scorpions and snakes in the undergrowth.

"I wish I could have brought his playpen or bouncer or crib, but we would have no room in this hut to put them."

"I know, Darling. This slatted wooden floor is not a safe place for our baby to crawl. When I come home for lunch and can sneak a short nap, I can lie on the bed and hold Zaw's ankle so he will not wander off the bed."

"What a good idea! I will have time to go outside the hut and do my chores quickly."

Zaw was content to move around within the parameters of the length of his sleeping Phay Phay's arms and was always quiet as he waited for me to return.

"Hello, my baby boy. You have been so good for your Phay Phay."

He would reach out his arms so I could cuddle him.

He was a bonny, bouncing baby, fair-skinned with jet-black hair, laughing and cooing when we played games with him.

"Peek-a-boo," I would say, as Pe would hide behind the bamboo partition. Then, we would look for Pe, and Zaw would let out a little squeal when he saw him. He had a sweet disposition and brought us so much joy.

"I am so glad our baby is so easy to care for. He just takes a nap on our bed, and when I need to get some indoor chores done, he cuddles with the little stuffed toy his grandmother gave him."

He could pull himself up, but for some reason, he never crawled on the floor of the hut, but only pushed himself around by sliding on his bottom.

"I don't think he likes the floor." Pe laughed. "I think he will go from pushing himself around straight to standing up and walking."

We'd go for long walks in the evening. Pe carried the baby as we had no strollers or prams. Although there were so many things we had to do without, those were happy days.

"I am so happy you have more time to spend with us now that your health assistant sometimes stays on-site at the hospital."

Pe came home early one day and laughed when he saw a bib around Zaw's neck and a mess of food around his lips.

"I couldn't buy baby food, so I cooked soft food and mashed it with a fork to give to him between nursing. Boiled eggs from our two chickens, mashed rice, and potatoes are his favorite foods. And he seems to be thriving on them."

God Will Protect Your Path

All this time in the jungle, Pe had made it a point that we sit on the floor beside our bed and read together from his worn Bible before we bowed in prayer. Then, as we lay in bed, he would tell me stories from the Bible that meant so much to him. He would explain Jesus' parables and share the prayers in the Bible written by Paul. It was so comforting to fall off to sleep with the promises he said were ours if we believe.

Now that we had Zaw, all three of us shared this precious time together. Sitting on our bed or lying down in our cozy bedroom, Pe shared stories from the Bible. "God made the light. He also made the sun, the moon, the stars, the animals, and the people." Pe tipped up Zaw's little chin. "And God made you, and God made May May too."

We didn't have any children's books to read, but Pe used his artistic talent to draw pictures of Bible stories. As Pe presented the illustrations, Zaw would clap his hands and smile. And I loved watching Pe lovingly instruct Zaw to put his hands together and close his eyes as he taught him how to pray.

I learned some kids' Bible songs that we sang along with other kids' songs I knew. We both loved clapping our hands to the tune of "If You're Happy and You Know It (Clap Your Hands)." Laughing and giggling, Zaw would fall off to sleep as we moved him to his little place against the wall on my side of the bed.

This was our family time and became our tradition as Pe continued leading us in times of prayer and worship.

Life had become sweeter, but soon, struggling to survive in this unsanitary place, where resigning was not an option, took its toll. We continued working, living, loving, and laughing in this place that had become our sanctuary, but after two long, hard years, we were continually tired and depleted.

"We haven't had a break, Darling. I wish I had more time for you and our baby." The health assistant was now on his motorcycle once again, going to the neighboring villages, and we suspected he was earning some payback while still working for the government, but we had no way of knowing for sure.

"Your work at the hospital is getting more and more exhausting, and life with a baby, when we have no baby food or normal things a baby needs, is getting harder by the day." There were no stores or open markets. We had to make do with weekly vendors who carried a few bony chickens and week-old vegetables.

I found solace in Pe's prayers and trust in his God, and I would hold on to his comforting words such as, "God wants us to trust Him with all our hearts. He will direct our paths if we depend on Him."

That same unseen hand, unknown by us, was at work. Soon, He brought an incident into our lives that moved us from where we were to a place we did not know.

Chapter 27

Speak to Me, Darling, Don't Go Away from Me

Before I formed you in the womb I knew you,
before you were born I set you apart.
–Jeremiah 1:5a NIV

But the pot he was shaping from the clay
was marred in his hands;
so the potter formed it into another pot,
shaping it as seemed best to him.
–Jeremiah 18:4 NIV

It was a Friday. It had rained all night, and the dark clouds were still ominous. I was up early. Zaw was restless and had kept me awake the whole night. The previous evening, he had thrown up his dinner, and I had to change his diaper at least twenty times during the night.

I looked over at Pe, who should already have been at work. His face was pale, and his breath seemed shallow. I felt his forehead, which was hot and clammy, and it woke him up.

With a slight smile, his glazed eyes looked up at me, and he said, "I'm thirsty."

"I'll get you some water, Darling."

I got up and gave him the murky water I had boiled the previous day, putting in a few tea leaves to make it palatable. I had finally gone into a deep sleep just before early dawn, so I did not hear him when he got out of bed several times and threw up at the window.

Then Zaw started to cry. And when I picked him up, I saw his forehead was puckered up, and his face was turning pale.

I heard moaning and turned to see Pe in a confused state of semi-consciousness. He needed acute medical care, but all I could do was stand beside his bed, holding our year-and-a-half-old son, who was suffering from the same virus. His normally plump little baby face and body were shriveled, and his eyes looked sunken and dull.

The rain beat against the tin roof. *Was it the monsoon, or was it the hammering of my heart?* I felt helpless. *Would I run out, holding my baby in the downpour when he was already sick? Or stay and watch my husband slip further into unconsciousness? How would I notify any of the villagers to get help?*

Lightning seemed to split the sky, lighting up the dark night for a second, but there was no help in sight.

Three days went by. No one visited our hut. We had no food or water, and there was no one besides myself to take care of my delirious husband and baby. I could only walk my baby back and forth, looking from his shriveled little face to my husband's still form as he lay in an almost semi-conscious state.

"I feel so helpless. I wish I could do something for you."

Pe did not respond.

"Speak to me, Darling, don't go away from me." By this time, I was sobbing as my eyes looked from his ashen face to our baby's body lying limply in my arms.

Just when I felt that both my husband and our son were going to slip away from me, a loud knock heralded the wife of the township officer. She came in and took in the scene, immediately radioing her husband.

"Get the doctors from Yin-ma-bin to come immediately. Our doctor and his child need immediate care."

We were then surrounded by villagers, who kneeled around Pe's bed, complaining of all their aches and pains. All while my husband lay curled up in a ball, suffering from severe dehydration caused by a violent attack of gastroenteritis that totally sapped his strength and energy.

Daw Aye shooed them away. "The doctor is sick. Please go back to your homes. We will take care of all of you as soon as we can."

She radioed her husband again, "Can you find out where the health assistant is? He needs to be here to take care of the patients."

I Couldn't Bear it if I Lost You

In what seemed a blur, the township doctor in a nearby town was radioed to come and pick us up in his jeep. We were carted off to their more sophisticated hospital complex, where I gave up my husband and child into their care and let myself fall off to sleep in utter exhaustion, knowing that, at last, I could let go and not have to remain strong for them.

Both husband and wife were medical doctors and took in the situation immediately. "Don't worry, Ma Ma Nita, we will look after your husband and your baby. You are exhausted and need to rest."

She took the baby in her arms, and my husband was wheeled off immediately into the room they used for patients needing intensive care.

The sheer exhaustion of the weekend shock and strain, coupled with the heat and lack of sleep and food, forced me to place the two people dearest to me into another's care as sleep overcame me. Pe and Zaw wrestled for their lives for the next few days.

We made it through the ordeal. Then, in his own jeep, the doctor took us back to the jetty in Monywa and waited for the next ferry to take us across. Once across, we traveled back in a bullock cart to Palai. Zaw was singing all along the dusty, bumpy roads, and my heart was thankful as I held him close. I had almost lost both my husband and my baby.

"I love you so much, Darling. I couldn't bear it if I lost you."

Pe put his arms around me and put his thin cheek next to mine, "God provided for us and protected us, and He has been with you and me and our baby this whole time."

Taking my hand and Zaw's hand in his, he closed his eyes and bowed his head. "Thank You, heavenly Father. You are *Jehovah Rapha*, our Rock, our Fortress, and our Strong Tower. You made us, and You took care of us and brought healing as we rested in You. We love You. In Jesus's name, Amen."

"Will you be all right to return to caring for the patients when we get home? You are still so weak. I wish you could rest for one more week."

We were sitting up in front on the slight ridge of the bullock cart, trying to hold each other steady. I glanced at Pe's face and saw how hollow his cheekbones had become.

"I will be okay if I can sleep through tonight. Don't worry, Darling. It's going to be okay. Thanks to the doctors who took care of us, not only are we going to make it through, but they have already wired a request for my transfer, and they have asked for an immediate release from my post here."

With the trauma to our family and the strong recommendations from the Yin-ma-bin doctors to the minister of health stating dire consequences to Pe's health if he continued serving in Palai, our request for a transfer came through. And although my husband was not given an appointment at Rangoon General Hospital, he was commissioned as the designated team leader for the World Health Organization Medical Team for the relief campaign for trachoma—a disease in the eye caused by the Chlamydia trachomatis bacterium that can cause irreversible blindness—in Meiktila, then a semi-developed town in central Burma,

We were thankful to leave Palai, where we had spent two years of our married life fighting to survive in primitive, dirty conditions. Though we later discovered we had been sent there as punishment for what the health government considered his brother's treason, we learned so many lessons along the way as we overcame countless obstacles and successfully managed to live without many necessities.

Through it all, Pe's faith remained strong. I watched him and wondered and thirsted for more of what he had in his faith. I did not know that, like the "deer that panted for streams of water," my soul was panting for the living God.

God, as the master Potter, was preparing the soil of my heart. He had been pursuing me for so long, and He graciously removed the clutter and debris that prevented me from seeing Him. Looking back now, I recognize that He had to put me through the long process of molding and shaping me into the vessel He had planned for me to be even before He formed me in my mother's womb.

Chapter 28

A Future and a Hope

*There is a strange statement in Scripture that flashes like a bright neon sign.
We see it when the author of the book of Hebrews speaks of Abraham
pulling up his lifelong roots from his hometown, Ur, and leaving
for—let's see, where was he going? Abraham didn't know!*
–Chuck Swindoll[1]

*By faith Abraham, when called to go to a place
he would later receive as his inheritance, obeyed and went,
even though he did not know where he was going.*
–Hebrews 11:8 NIV

Meiktila, Burma, January 1970

In Meiktila, we were given a real brick house. With electricity. And running water. I still had to carry buckets of water into the house from the outdoor faucet, but we had water. I had an attached kitchen sporting a single, very primitive stove, but there was no danger of it floating off in a flood.

We still had an outhouse, and I still dreaded the experience, but at least it was close by and in our own fenced yard.

"This is wonderful, Sweetheart. I am glad we went through the worst, and now it is all behind us. I think we will be able to make a nice home here."

I could tell that Pe was very happy working with the World Health Organization Medical Team. He came home from his first day of work elated and on top of the world.

"Darling, I cannot believe this. The hospital is top-notch. It is equipped with all the staff, equipment, instruments, and supplies I need."

I looked at my sweet husband, so grateful he was finally experiencing some relief. For two years, he had accepted such difficult circumstances, working with whatever he had in the hospital in Palai and making the best of a situation that nobody should ever have to be in.

Pe discovered a Christian church just a few blocks from our home. It was a beautiful building at the edge of Meiktila Lake. Each Sunday, we would take Zaw's hand and walk to church. I loved sitting in the pew between Pe and Zaw. The beautiful music sung by the church choir reminded me of the hymns we used to sing in chapel at the Methodist English High School in my kindergarten through high school years. Walking back home along the lake was so peaceful. And every evening, Zaw and I looked forward to listening to Pe read our family devotions.

I was happy to join Pe in his religion, and three weeks after we first attended, I took part in a baptism they held in the lake. I thought that now I would truly be a Christian.

Life was now uneventful. Pe had been given a leadership position at the hospital and worked well with the eye doctors in the relief campaign for trachoma in Meiktila. Every day was a joy for him. "Darling, I not only get to treat the patients who are suffering from trachoma, but I get to do eye surgery as well." During his time with the campaign, he was able to perform thousands of eye surgeries, including cataract procedures, which were his first love.

We built lasting relationships with the doctors and their wives. It was like a balm to our worn-out bodies and minds. "I have so missed being with other couples, Darling," Pe said. "Isn't it wonderful to be with friends to share our hopes and dreams with?" He put his arms around me. "I have felt sad that you had to be so isolated in Palai, and I am thankful that God brought us to a larger place. You must be so happy to have a real kitchen and stove and lots of rooms in our red brick house."

"Yes, and I feel thankful that I no longer have to wait for a seventh-day open market but can walk to the local market across the railway lines, carrying my shopping basket."

We had learned to appreciate the things that middle-class and wealthy people often take for granted.

Look Out, World! I'm Here

Another bright spot in our lives was that Zaw was able to go to kindergarten with the other children. He was now a healthy and happy little boy, so accepting of wherever he was.

I became pregnant with our second child, a surprise I wanted to share with Pe on a day we were out at the Meiktila Lake.

"I have news, Darling."

He pulled me close and said, "I think I know."

We whispered to each other, "We are going to have another baby!"

Even Zaw was excited as we prepared for his new sister or brother. "When is the baby coming? Will I get to look after the baby?"

All went well with the pregnancy. However, I did develop amoebic dysentery during the last months, which I had probably caught during our time in Palai. This condition, coupled with the fact that I had a three-year-old son to care for, drained my energy, leaving me feeling lethargic and tired. This subsided, however, and we looked forward to our baby's birth with joy.

"I'm so happy that we won't have to travel and go through what we did for Zaw to be born."

Pe chuckled. "I was playing golf with an old friend last week, one of the attending MDs at the military hospital here in Meiktila. She said she would make sure you got admitted there. Of course, it's a very up-to-date medical unit, as all the military wives have their babies there."

It was there in Meiktila that our daughter Mimi was born, this time in a hygienic, modern facility. Pe would laughingly tell people. "Mimi came into this world like a little ray of sunshine. If she had been born with a tiny trumpet and knew how to use it, I think she would have tooted it to let the whole world know *I'm here!*"

God gave us two children, so different from each other yet so amazing in character and strength, and we could not have wished for anything more.

It was easier now to visit my parents and sisters and to see Pe's father as well. Our children enjoyed spending time with their grandparents and aunts, and we did so more often as it brought so much joy to them all. Our two children and I would travel by train to Rangoon, and on the way, the two would excitedly tell other passengers, "We are going to see Pho Pho and Grandma and Aunty Esme and Aunty Gail and Aunty Chicky. Then we will see our Phay Phay's Daddy."

My parents were preparing to emigrate to Sydney, Australia, with my sisters, and we made the most of the time we had left together.

Chapter 29

It Is Time

The Lord had said to Abram,
"Go from your country, your people and your father's household
to the land I will show you."
–Genesis 12:1 NIV

There is a time for everything,
and a season for every activity under the heavens:
a time to be born and a time to die,
a time to plant and a time to uproot.
–Ecclesiastes 3:1–2 NIV

Terror upon terror suddenly befell us as, unannounced, the military police barged into our family's country home. They handcuffed Daddy and escorted him to prison just hours before his scheduled departure for Sydney, Australia.

When my father returned from the ordeal, he was dark-eyed and gaunt. After being ruthlessly taken away, he had been interrogated, coerced, and confined for days on trumped-up charges.

"Nita, it was horrible," Gail said. "Several uniformed and armed officers came in and took Daddy away. Three other men turned literally everything

in our house upside down and even tried to get Chicky, who was sick, to
get up so they could search her bed."

We could sense the terror that Daddy must have felt as he was held prisoner.
"Tita and Pe, they held a flashlight to my eyes while they questioned me
without any mercy. There was no rhyme or reason why they should have
locked me up. I was tortured for three days and three nights and only
released when the London head office of the P&O Lines paid the huge
ransom this dictator government held over my head." He shook his head
in disbelief. "Their story was that P&O owed me back vacation pay and
the Burmese income tax office here should have collected on the taxes.
P&O did not owe me any vacation pay. It was all lies in order to get money
from the London office." He sighed. "My passport and all my papers were
confiscated."

After that, my father, mother, and sisters—Gail and Chicky—were detained for another year.

Other incidents also occurred. Underground student activism and open
mass student involvement in national politics had erupted during the student protests of the mid-1970s, while we had been away from Rangoon.

My native country was being torn apart. The economy plunged. Socialized
medicine forced people to wait in long lines. Sick people had to sleep on
mats in hospital corridors because there were not enough beds. And there
were not enough drugs to go around.

Yes, education, health, and welfare were free, but at what cost? The military government took absolute control, degrading the people's spirits and
finally demolishing and snuffing out their morale. The rich still survived,
for almost any material thing could be bought with money, but even
their dreams were broken as socialism marched on insidiously and tore
everything down that they had built or held dear.

As we got ready for bed that night, Pe said, "I think it is time to leave Burma."

"Yes, I was thinking the same thing."

"The army government is stretching its powerful claws, and this is no place for our children to grow up. Armed guards are everywhere. We never know if our telephone lines are being tapped, and we know that whatever we say will be held against us. Military Intelligence Service is at every function."

It was well known that diamonds, rubies, star sapphires, gems, and precious stones were all being siphoned into Swiss banks by the military elite government. There was no more freedom—and certainly no freedom of speech.

A few more of our lifelong family friends were taken into solitary confinement with no trial. Others were interrogated and marked. Many had risked their lives to cross the border.

"Ko Thet was telling me that Ko Tu had to leave Jenny, their two small daughters, his parents and siblings, and his law practice and escape to Bangkok and finally to the United States."

Ko Tu was Pe's childhood friend—the one who had made it possible for Pe and me to meet. Jenny, my cousin and childhood hide-and-go-seek companion, escaped through the jungle with her two small daughters and reunited with him after eight years, making a home near Washington, DC.

The "brain drain" of professionals began as Burma could no longer be home to an educated, elite class. Many of our classmates and friends emigrated to different parts of the world—England, America, Australia, Singapore, Hong Kong, and India, to name a few places.

Pe's older brother, Patrick, had taken a position as an eye surgeon with the World Health Organization in Aleppo, and he and Ann, with their two young children, had already left Burma.

Pe had been in fervent prayer for God to guide his steps and waited patiently for His leading as plans to immigrate had begun to formulate after his sister had strongly advised him to join her in America. "Ma Ma Patricia moved to New York about ten years ago, and she is now the Deputy Director at the United Nations Development Program. She has sent our plane tickets and has helped secure a bona fide job for me in New York. It is time for us to leave Meiktila. What do you think about us moving there?"

"Well, we've already decided to leave our country," I said. "I will start tomorrow morning to send in our application for visas to the American Consulate in Rangoon."

The moment we put in our applications to leave our homeland of Burma, Pe was forced to resign from his government position. Undaunted, he opened a private practice adjacent to our Meiktila house. Before long, money flowed in as patients came to see him for treatment.

"The government is demonetizing all the money in the banks. Let's hide these stacks of money under our bed. There is no more room in the suitcase you brought me."

Although we could not see it at that time, Pe later said that was God's way of making sure we would have enough money to appease the greedy military government at our departure.

We received our USA visas almost immediately from the head of the American Consulate. "Here, Pe, in this packet are individual Social Security cards for both of you and for your two small children."

Not knowing what we would use them for, my husband initially declined the Social Security cards. However, that wise man persuaded us to take them. "I give you my word that your dictator government will not hear about it from me."

Little did we know that hundreds of people were waiting in line to get work permits so they could work in the United States of America. But God had already gone before us, paving the way.

Daddy, Mummy, and my two sisters were still waiting for the renewal of their passports, even though it had been almost a year since the government had confiscated them. My older sister, Esme, was married by then and had decided to remain in Rangoon.

As for us, we had no idea what awaited us. We would be leaving family, friends, and everything near and dear to us. But God had already planned our steps.

Pe, like Abraham, was going to leave a place he knew and loved, obeying his God and following where He led, without knowing where he was going but trusting in the One who would care for Him. Every night, as he led our family in prayer, Pe would assert his faith by closing with, "Father, Your will be done."

Part IV

From Golden Pagodas to Land of Liberty

Chapter 30

Welcome, my Darlings, Welcome

See, I am doing a new thing!
Now it springs up; do you not perceive it?
I am making a way in the wilderness
and streams in the wasteland.
–Isaiah 43:19 NIV

Rangoon Airport, November 2, 1973

The time had come. With bated breath, we started walking quickly on the tarmac and immediately boarded the BOAC jet plane waiting there. We dared not look back to see if the two men with the revolvers were following us.

I finally sneaked a nervous peek behind to see if I would recognize either of them. They were nowhere to be seen. Perhaps they were already seated in first class and had gone ahead, or perhaps they had not yet boarded and were going to have us taken off the plane once we were in the cabin. My heart was thumping.

Pe took both my hands, which were still shaking as we got on the plane and took our seats. He bowed his head and prayed, "Dear Lord, You have protected us thus far. Please give us a safe flight. We give You our journey, our arrival, and our move to this distant land You are taking us to. Let Your way be our way, and Your purpose be our purpose. In Jesus' name."

My fears settled as his gentle voice soothed and calmed me. I looked over and saw the children asleep and fastened snugly into their seats. They were exhausted. Pe still held my hands, and I closed my eyes. Peace gently washed over me.

After what seemed like forever, the propeller roared to life and the plane began to move— lifting into the sky with the wheels retracting. Then we felt peace. We sat back with thankfulness. We would not be held back by the dictator government. Pent-up tears poured down my cheeks, and Pe gently wiped them.

Little Mimi was still asleep, but Zaw woke up as soon as the plane took off. His eyes were round with excitement. His little five-year-old body seemed to relax as he sat back in his seat.

"They did let us go, Phay Phay. Your prayers were answered."

"Yes, Thar Thar, let's thank Him now and ask Him to take us safely all the way to America. It won't take us long to get to our first stop."

We changed planes in Bangkok, Thailand. It was not until we landed at the airport that we could finally grasp the fact we had escaped the fear and tyranny and were now entering freedom. The week had been tense, alternating between despair and hope, but now it was over. And our hearts were bursting with sighs of relief as we slowly exhaled.

Our emotions had been raw, not knowing whether we would get our papers and be able to catch the flight out the same night even though we had open tickets. The rest of the ordeal was now a blur, but we felt the release of tension that comes only when we've climbed the mountain in front of us, which once seemed unsurmountable, and have reached the other side.

"It's going to be a long journey, Darling. Our itinerary is from Rangoon to Bangkok, then on to Calcutta and Kuwait, with a short stop in London, and finally to the United States of America." Pe kept up with the time changes as we moved back in time.

We held hands through each flight. He smiled at me. "My hands will hold yours for as long as I live. I will never let you go."

I fell asleep through most of the flights, and so did our children. Each time I woke up, Pe's head was bowed in prayer. He had taken his family away, leaving everything we had known and cherished, and I knew he was entrusting us into his heavenly Father's care.

It was all so final. We had waited two years to get our papers so we could leave our own country. We had signed documents that denounced us as traitors and paid the government five years' income tax in advance and twenty thousand kyats each before we could leave. But now, those terrible moments seemed to have occurred eons ago. My fingers felt bare. I had been forced to leave my rings and my jewelry. I fingered the twenty-dollar bill in my bag. That was all we were allowed, but it was all worth it to finally be free.

The journey was long and hard—a total of twenty-seven hours on flights. And it was not until we arrived in New York that we felt completely safe.

We arrived at John F. Kennedy Airport at 7 p.m. on the night of November 3, 1973, where we were welcomed by my sister-in-law, Patricia, her husband, Roy, and their two sons, John and Sam.

Pe had always been emotional when telling what his sister had meant to him. "We lost our mother when I was thirteen years old. Ma Ma is five years older than me and has always taken care of me. She left for America when I was eighteen."

And now I met her. Tears welled in my eyes as I watched Patricia hug her little brother.

"Oh, Son Son Lay, you are here. You are finally here." In a voice gone husky, tears streaming down her beautiful face, she whispered, "Welcome, darlings, welcome." She included the children and me in a group hug.

We drove to Manhattan, New York, where Patricia and her family lived. As Roy opened the door to their home, he said, "Nita and Son, this is your home now until we get you settled into a home of your own."

Mixed feelings came in floods—gratitude for Roy and Pat's generous hearts rolled up with relief, joy, exhaustion, sadness, trepidation, and so many other emotions. We were embarking on an unknown journey, and who knew what was ahead for our fledgling family of four?

There's No Place for You

When we had put in our application to the Burmese immigration office two years earlier, Pe received a job offer, but that no longer existed. Now, with no money and completely dependent on his sister and her big-hearted husband, I silently suffered for my gentle, precious Pe. In the wintery, blustery cold of November, he tramped the streets of New York in custom-made shoes that now threatened to fall apart with the miles he put on them, looking for a hospital that would provide him with an internship.

He would come home after each long day, shaking his head and saying, "All the hospitals I went to have their full quota of doctors."

"Why can't you join a group of doctors, Son Son?" Roy questioned. "You've practiced medicine and surgery for more than five years. Pat said you were the medical team leader for the trachoma campaign with the World Health Organization and passed the American board exam for foreign medical graduates."

"That's true, Roy, but our British-equivalent medical degree is not immediately reciprocal in the United States. It is accepted only in England and countries where the British medical degree is recognized."

Roy shook his head.

"However, I am only required to repeat the internship year, and it is a difficult position to place in November as most of the hospitals hold only two open internship spots each in January and July."

One evening Patricia, watching her brother lying back on the sofa with his forehand on his brow, sat beside him and said, "Son Son, how can you be so calm? I am so worried for you."

Pe put his arm around her. "Ma Ma, God has already planned out His path for us. His word says in Philippians 4:6–7, 'Do not be anxious about anything, but in every situation, by prayer and petition, with thanksgiving, present your requests to God. And the peace of God, which transcends all understanding, will guard your hearts and minds in Christ Jesus.'"

She nodded. "Are there other hospitals that you could reach out to?"

"Well, one of the physicians who interviewed me said that an intern vacancy just opened up at Washington General Hospital."

"Go tomorrow, Son Son. I'll get your train ticket for Washington, DC."

Pe returned home late that night. "Washington General Hospital offered me a place in July of 1974, but that is eight months away, and I couldn't take it."

With a family of four and no money to support us, Pe never gave up. Night after night, as he prayed, he claimed his life's verses, which I had heard so many times that I had memorized them. Like, "Trust in the Lord with all your heart and do not lean on your own understanding. In all your ways acknowledge Him, and He will direct your paths." And "Seek first His kingdom and His righteousness, and all these things will be given to you as well."

We spent Christmas in New York, where we had a beautiful reunion with Patrick and his family after their decision to leave Aleppo and emigrate to the United States.

We sent Pe's resume all over the United States, even to Alaska. His prayers were answered as God, with a mighty hand, moved us from New York to Chattanooga, Tennessee—straight into the Bible Belt. Erlanger Hospital accepted his application and sent our family plane tickets to travel on December 31, 1973.

We packed our one suitcase, kissed his sister and her family goodbye at LaGuardia airport, and flew through Atlanta to the Chattanooga Metropolitan Airport. Patricia had given us enough money for the taxi, which carried us to the entrance of what was to become our new home.

In New York, we had been with family, and the culture there, though a thousand times more fast-paced, was similar to the old Rangoon in many ways. Now, we traveled hundreds of miles south into unknown territory for a new adventure. And although we discovered later that there were very few ethnic groups there at that time, Chattanooga became our home.

I could tell Pe was excited; he looked forward to working, learning, and healing. This was his calling.

Joy in any circumstance! Hope in our hearts! Freedom beckoned! With wide-open arms, we embraced the unknown. Our struggles to survive became opportunities to thrive. As Pe always said, our disappointments become God's appointments.

Every corner we turned would be a new adventure. With our arms entwined around each other, our two-year-old daughter, and our son—who was not yet six—we stepped out and met the challenges. With complete calmness and serenity, Pe faced this new adventure, trusting in God for the outcome.

And what challenges, what encounters, what outcomes would come as a result of being uprooted, of being planted in foreign soil? Little did we know how colorful our life would become as we put down stakes in the great state of Tennessee.

Chapter 31

Lift Your Empty Hands to Me

One by one He took them from me,
All the things I valued most,
Until I was empty-handed;
Every glittering toy was lost.

And I walked earth's highways, grieving.
In my rags and poverty.
Till I heard His voice inviting,
"Lift your empty hands to Me!"

So I held my hands toward heaven,
And He filled them with a store
Of His own transcendent riches,
Till they could contain no more.

And at last I comprehended
With my stupid mind and dull,
That God COULD not pour His riches
Into hands already full!
–Martha Snell Nicholson[1]

December 31, 1973, Chattanooga, Tennessee

We got out of the taxi and followed Pe down the outside staircase of an apartment building. The side door opened into an unfurnished basement apartment. Looking out, all we saw were the feet of people and pets as they walked past our sorry excuse for windows, which were just slits high up near the ceiling. We were now in our own home in our adopted land, and we were literally starting out at the bottom.

This was not how I expected our new life to begin. True, it was a million times better than our Palai hut. But even our Meiktila two-storied home had more space and more windows—and was a far cry from this tiny, one-bedroom basement apartment.

I spoke to my quaking heart. *You are free here in America, Nita, free from bondage and tyranny, free to build your own life.* I grabbed hold of Pe's hand.

Zaw and Mimi ran into the small place and climbed excitedly up onto the window ledge to look out to the parking lot.

Pe held out his hands, "Come Thar Thar and Thamee Lay, let's thank Jesus for bringing us to this home."

With little hands tightly held in ours, our eyes met as we bowed our heads. Pe prayed. "Please bless this home, Jesus. We love You and thank You." We held each other tight as we all ended with, "Amen."

Pe prepared me right at the beginning, "I'm going to have to work every other night as well, Darling. As a first-year intern, I am required to be on alternate night call."

He was paid for a forty-hour week, but he worked eighty-eight hours a week. I would only see him every second night. And on the nights he came home, the children were already asleep by the time he arrived.

Zaw was missing his daddy. "Can we stay up tonight until Phay Phay comes home?" "Not tonight, Sweetheart. Today is Wednesday, and tomorrow is a school day. I know he must leave before five-thirty in the morning and will have to work until 8 p.m. on Saturday, but maybe Saturday night we can have a surprise dinner ready for him. Won't that be fun?"

We slept on the floor with just the three blankets we had brought from Patricia's home. Pe thanked Jesus that there was a carpet on the bedroom floor so that we could use the blankets for a covering.

Zaw brought in some empty cardboard boxes he found discarded in the hallway.

"Thank you, Thar Thar. Look, Mimi, we can use these cardboard boxes for our dining table. Aunty Pat gave us a pretty tablecloth."

I washed and rewashed the six plates, cups, and silverware that Patricia had bought us in New York and the small frying pan given to us by a neighbor who lived directly above us.

We struggled to make ends meet with Pe's pay rate of $2.65 an hour as an intern at Erlanger Hospital.

"I paid the rent today. And I figured out that every month we will be left with forty dollars for food, clothing, medicine, and bus fares."

Pe hugged me from behind as I stood at the sink, washing the little frying pan, and he put his chin on my head. "You always make do."

I giggled, "We can survive if we make do with just the bare necessities." The two of us had already learned that in our one-room shack in Palai.

Without our own means of transportation or even an umbrella to shelter us from the rain or heat, Pe took two different buses and walked a long distance to get to his job at the hospital. And I would walk with the children to the closest grocery store. We couldn't buy much, but I made a game of it with the kids, having fun as we walked down the aisles. "Bananas, no! Eggs, no!" And, "Look, May May, we were able to buy a small packet of ground beef, a tiny bag of rice, a handful of potatoes, and a small carton of milk for the entire week. Aren't we brilliant?"

"That's right, Thar Thar." I looked at Zaw, who had been counting as we shopped. We would walk out of the grocery store with our one paper bag holding our groceries on the little stroller Roy had bought for Mimi and head home.

Pe's World

With a twenty-hour continuing shift, Pe could only be home every second night from 8 p.m. to 6 a.m. "I know the hours are long, Darling, and I'm actually repeating the rotating internship training I received before we got married, but it has been a very interesting experience being in the emergency room of an American hospital."

Pe never complained, but I knew those added nights were hard on him. I would find him asleep as I prepared his dinner, having to wake him up so he could eat. The children hardly saw him, and he missed most of their church and school functions until he had completed his internship and was accepted into the residency program.

Even though we had left everything and everyone we knew, we never gave up and worked hard to survive. Fear and oppression and tyranny were things of the past, and we were grateful for what we had even as we struggled for those four years as Pe completed his year of internship and three years of ophthalmology residency.

Yes, it was true that we had been forced to wait two long years before the Burmese government would let us leave, and as far as the world's goods, we had nothing. Yet as we stepped onto the shores of America, we had stepped into freedom from fear. But more special than that, I stepped into a world I knew existed but did not know well.

I had never stopped searching, looking for that elusive something to fill that constant hole in my heart. In Meiktila, I had thought that getting baptized in the lake by the church would make me the Christian I expected to become. But going through that ritual did not fill the void that was still in my heart. So I knew there had to be something more.

But God was already at work, and I stepped into Pe's world.

Chapter 32

Exodus and the Red Sea Road

"Then you will call on me and come and pray to me,
and I will listen to you.
You will seek me and find me
when you seek me with all your heart.
I will be found by you," declares the LORD,
"and will bring you back from captivity."
–Jeremiah 29:12–14 NIV

Pe met Melissa, a medical librarian at the hospital campus. She came to our basement home to help settle us in. She gave us two cans of baked beans, but we did not have a can opener. So I stored the cans until we could afford a can opener.

Later she saw the cans sitting on a shelf in our pantry. "Why on earth didn't you tell me? I'll go out and buy you one right now." Besides a can opener, she bought us plastic bowls and a few other necessary kitchen items.

We literally had no pots and only a single pan to our name, but we had peace and profound joy.

Our children learned to do without as they played with cardboard boxes for toys or made chains out of scrap paper. They were such happy children and were content with what little we possessed.

"Look what we made, May May. This is for you and Phay Phay. It says Happy Anniversary. Let's hang it on the door so he will see it when he comes home."

They had used the scrap paper from the apartment complex office and the coloring pencils that Melissa had brought them.

My Breakthrough

After we had been settled in our new home for four months, Melissa dropped by late one evening. "Why don't you, Dr. Tin, and the children come to my church this Sunday? I teach Sunday School for the five- to six-year-olds and could keep Zaw and Mimi with me."

She drove us to a small stone church with a tiny sanctuary that was packed with people.

The pastor's message was titled "Egypt in our Hearts." As he spoke about the miracle at the Red Sea and God's children crossing over, it struck something in my searching heart. It finally dawned on me that even though I had joined a church and gotten baptized in Meiktila, I was still in bondage and had, figuratively, "never left Egypt." That was the reason I had never felt set free in my spirit.

As I sat on the pew in deep thought, I realized that, like the children of Israel who had been in bondage to the Pharoah, I had been in bondage to the religion I was brought up in. I finally understood I had been living under a works doctrine and had not gotten rid of the belief that I had to work my way to heaven. But the worst part was that I still didn't know how to get there.

So, I continued to listen intently.

The pastor read a passage from Isaiah. "I provide water in the wilderness and streams in the wasteland, to give drink to my people, my chosen, the people I formed for myself that they may proclaim my praise" (Isaiah 43:20b–21 NIV). The lady sitting next to me opened her Bible and shared it with me.

I remembered my husband reading Psalm 91 and telling me that God would provide and protect His children. It was something I had clung to. But this verse was new to me. Here, God was calling them *His* people, *His* chosen, and the people that *He* had formed. And He said He was also providing for them in the wilderness and in the wastelands.

But, "chosen"? That reminded me of Mrs. Emma Smith-Jones' tapestry. *I have loved you with an everlasting love, therefore with loving kindness I have drawn you.* Before a drawing, there had to be a choosing. How amazing!

The pastor then spoke from Exodus 13:17–18. "When Pharaoh let the people go, God did not lead them on the road through the Philistine country, though that way was shorter. For God said, 'If they face war, they might change their minds and return to Egypt.' So God led the people around by the desert road toward the Red Sea."

The pastor stopped and looked at us. "Our heavenly Father will not only provide for us, His children, but He will also lead us. Look in the Scriptures at how He went before the children of Israel. 'By day the LORD went ahead of them in a pillar of cloud to guide them on their way and by night in a pillar of fire to give them light, so that they could travel by day or night.

Neither the pillar of cloud by day nor the pillar of fire by night left its place in front of the people'" (Exodus 13:21–22 NIV).

"This message is for us today. You may not have an Egyptian army behind you, but are you facing your own Red Sea? Are you wondering how you can get across? And once across, do you know the road you need to be on? Let's read Exodus 14 beginning at verse 10."

The lady sitting beside me turned the page and pointed to the place in her Bible so I could read it with her.

> *As Pharaoh approached, the Israelites looked up, and there were the Egyptians, marching after them. They were terrified and cried out to the LORD. They said to Moses, "Was it because there were no graves in Egypt that you brought us to the desert to die? What have you done to us by bringing us out of Egypt? Didn't we say to you in Egypt, 'Leave us alone; let us serve the Egyptians'? It would have been better for us to serve the Egyptians than to die in the desert!" (Exodus 14:10–12 NIV).*

"God is showing us today that He not only makes a way out, but He provides for a road-through for the children He is drawing to Himself."

> *Moses answered the people, "Do not be afraid. Stand firm and you will see the deliverance the LORD will bring you today. The Egyptians you see today you will never see again. The LORD will fight for you; you need only to be still."*
> *Then the LORD said to Moses, "Why are you crying out to me? Tell the Israelites to move on. Raise your staff and stretch out your hand over the sea to divide the water so that the Israelites*

can go through the sea on dry ground..."
Then the angel of God, who had been traveling in front of
Israel's army, withdrew and went behind them. The pillar of
cloud also moved from in front and stood behind them, coming
between the armies of Egypt and Israel. Throughout the night
the cloud brought darkness to the one side and light to the other
side; so neither went near the other all night long.
Then Moses stretched out his hand over the sea, and all that
night the LORD drove the sea back with a strong east wind
and turned it into dry land. The waters were divided, and the
Israelites went through the sea on dry ground, with a wall of
water on their right and on their left (Exodus 14:13–22 NIV).

The pastor's voice rang out with passion. "It was not their battle. God
wanted them to trust that He would deliver them and protect them. He
wanted them to believe that He would provide their way out and that they
would know without any doubt that they could rest in His deliverance and
His provision as He parted the Red Sea for them so that the waves became
a huge wall on either side to allow them to walk on dry ground and get
safely to the other side."

"Here is something else that I want you to see. Look at the way His presence
was with them all the way through their journey from their captivity to
freedom from their bondage."

He read verses 19 and 20 again, which were underlined in the lady's Bible.

Then the angel of God, who had been traveling in front of
Israel's army, withdrew and went behind them. The pillar of
cloud also moved from in front and stood behind them, coming
between the armies of Egypt and Israel. Throughout the night

the cloud brought darkness to the one side and light to the
other side; so neither went near the other all night long.

"Do you see what happened here? The angel of God moved from the front of Israel's army to the back so that Israel would have a shield between them and the Egyptians. The pillar of cloud also moved and gave them covering, as well as providing light for their path. The pillar of cloud was lit up so they could see their way in the dark."

He came to the end of his message. "If you're still in Egypt, if you've come to your own Red Sea and can't get across, God will make a way for you to follow His way and will come and meet you."

As soon as the message ended, I went with Melissa to speak to the pastor about the questions going around in my mind.

He nodded. "I understand. Let Melissa help you through a study book called *The Assurance of the Believer* that will answer your questions. He told Melissa to pick up the book from the library. She visited my home every day after work, and we went through the study together.

The Most Perfect Gift of All

On Day Two of my study, I came to the realization that it was not by joining a church, getting baptized, or leaning on my husband's faith that I would find the One my heart sought for. Like the Bible verse on Mrs. Emma Smith-Jones' wall, God *already* loved me with an everlasting love. All throughout my childhood and into my adult life, He had been drawing me with His loving kindness, but I had never opened my heart to Him.

One hundred and forty-six days after we set foot on this land we had been brought to, the eternal God, through His Holy Word in 1 John 5:11–13 finally drew me to Himself—a Scripture that has become indelible on my heart: "And this is the record, that God hath given to us eternal life, and this life is in his Son. He that hath the Son hath life; and he that hath not the Son of God hath not life. These things have I written unto you that believe on the name of the Son of God; that ye may know that ye have eternal life, and that ye may believe on the name of the Son of God" (KJV).

God, the master Potter, had brought me thus far. Throughout my life—including my childhood, teen, and young adult years—I had searched for that elusive peace and had sought it fervently with my whole heart. Now it was time! God had opened my heart to His Word, and I began to understand that it was not *religion* that Pe had but a *relationship* with his heavenly Father.

I wanted what he had, and in the early hours of my thirtieth birthday, I knelt on the kitchen floor and trustingly took the unconditional love God so freely offered me through the sacrificial death of His only Son on the cross. "Dear Jesus, thank You for saving me. Please come into my heart and my life. I love You." As the Holy Spirit of God opened my eyes and introduced me to my Savior, I found total and perfect freedom in the same God my husband worshipped.

My Jesus broke the shackles that held me captive and set me gloriously free. No longer was I afraid of the unseen spirits that had plagued me all my childhood, for perfect love had cast out fear. As I got up from my knees, I finally knew the peace that surpasses all understanding. I had, at last, found Him whom my soul had sought and longed for.

I looked at the kitchen clock. It was one minute after midnight on March 29, 1974—my thirtieth birthday. I had been given the gift of my Savior, the most perfect gift of all. How amazing that my physical birthday and my spiritual birthday fell on the same date, thirty years apart.

The answer I had been searching for was mine at last—peace *with* God and the peace *of* God! And that peace would overflow into our home and the lives He allowed us to touch.

I tried to slip quietly into bed so as not to wake Pe, but he was awake and waiting for me. He drew me close to him.

I whispered, "Darling, I asked Jesus to save me."

"I know," he kissed my cheeks, and both of our cheeks were wet with tears. "I have been praying for so long for you, and now our hearts are knit together totally in Him. I lay here in bed asking Jesus to open your heart to Him."

We were totally one now as we went to sleep in each other's arms.

God's Own Planting

Melissa called early the next morning. "So, what happened after I left last night?"

I was ecstatic. "You knew, didn't you? How on earth did you guess that I was going to receive Jesus as my Savior?"

"Your mind was going a mile a minute last night as we finished that second chapter in our study book, and you had so many questions. I somehow knew that it would happen. I am so happy. This is what Dr. Tin and I have been praying for."

I was just a tiny shoot that had grown up in a myriad of religions, but I was a planting of the Lord, and I was ready now for Him to grow me into a tree of His own choosing.

I wanted to know more; I wanted to know Jesus more. Something felt alive in me. Deep in my soul, my thirst had been quenched. Yet now I thirsted for more.

What was that verse on the decorative wooden plaque that Melissa and I admired when she took me to the Salvation Army store? I wrote it down on a piece of paper because it had piqued my attention. The painting was of a deer with liquid brown eyes beside a flowing stream where the ripples glistened in a beam of the sun's rays through a lush green forest. It mesmerized me, and the beautiful calligraphy brought up long-forgotten emotions of being drawn to Mrs. Emma Smith-Jones' oil painting hanging in her drawing room.

I pulled the paper out of the kitchen drawer. "As the deer pants for streams of water, so my soul pants for you, my God. My soul thirsts for God, for the living God. When can I go and meet with God?" (Psalm 42:1–2 NIV).

Pe came in just then. "What's going on in that cute little head of yours?"

"Isn't it amazing that God would love me so much and draw me to Himself so that I would long to know Him more?"

"Yes, and He will reveal Himself more and more as you read His Word. I can't wait for you to discover more. God says that if you seek Him with all your heart, you will find Him."

A few weeks later, my friend Wanda took me to a Bible study. It was a place where I was shown how to study the Bible for myself. And over the next more than forty years, Kay Arthur, the co-founder of Precept Ministries International,[1] was my Bible teacher and mentor. God poured into my life as I submersed myself in His Word, and my hungry heart was filled. I found what I had been seeking, but I discovered there was so much more than I had ever imagined.

These memories have paled with the years. And now, as I think of America—our "new" land for the last five decades—I praise God that it is the land where He gave me a new heart, a new life, a new spirit, a new family, and a new song. But above all, it is where He gave me Himself. As God said to Abraham in Genesis 15:1, "I am thy shield and thy exceeding great reward" (KJV). No other treasure could take the place of my God. So much lay in store for me as a child of the King.

Chapter 33

Overwhelmed by Kindness

True contentment is not having everything,
but in being satisfied with everything you have.
–Oscar Wilde.[1]

I am not saying this because I am in need,
for I have learned to be content whatever the circumstances.
I know what it is to be in need,
and I know what it is to have plenty.
I have learned the secret of being content
in any and every situation,
whether well fed or hungry,
whether living in plenty or in want.
I can do all this through him who gives me strength.
–Philippians 4:11-13 NIV

We did not have a car for two years, and when we eventually bought an old one for two hundred dollars, the radiator constantly leaked. "I'll patch it up with a cake of soap. A butane torch costs twenty-nine dollars." Every week, Pe would patiently patch the radiator. He took care of the car so well that it faithfully kept running for the next two years.

The Humped Mattress and a Singer

God provided in ways that we could not have known. We were still sleeping on the floor because we had no furniture when Melissa took us to her neighbor's, "They have a queen-size mattress in their garage," she said. "But it is old and stained."

Pe brought a small discarded surgical instrument with a pick at the end and pulled out the threads so we could remove the mattress cover to wash it. But when he came home later, he found me in the otherwise empty living room sitting on the humped-up mattress with his heavy medical books lying on the corners as I attempted in vain to get it flattened.

"You look exhausted, Darling. What happened to the mattress?"

"The cover washed clean and smelled nice, but it took me two hours to push the mattress back into its cover because it shrunk in the washing machine."

So Pe sat on the mattress while I jumped up and down on it. Then, the children joined us, and we ended up in hysterics. Finally, our joint efforts tamed that unwilling mattress.

Another friend gave us his old, scruffy recliner. "It needs its cover replaced, but you can have it if you want."

Several months later, we were given an old hide-a-bed sofa. The arm-chair that went along with it also needed some loving attention.

I had saved up for months for a little loveseat, and I was finally able to buy one that needed re-covering for five dollars. I cleaned it as much as possible, but we had no money to have it covered.

"I wish I had my sewing machine here. I could sew covers for all these old furniture pieces. Can't you see this little loveseat covered in gold velvet?"

Pe touched me under the chin. "My little seamstress, I know that if you had a sewing machine, you would make it fit for a prince and princess to sit on."

Then one evening, to my delight and surprise, Melissa brought me an old sewing machine. My jaw dropped open.

"Wow, a *Singer* sewing machine with a foot pedal. I used to sew on one when I was in my teens."

"This was just sitting in the corner of my neighbor's basement. She said you could have it."

"Oh, Melissa. I cannot thank you enough."

I found some gold velvet and royal blue and gold Jacobean patterned upholstery material suitable for my projects. Miraculously, the ten dollars-a-yard material was marked down to one dollar and fifty cents. I could not believe it.

I started making covers for all the furniture—what a rewarding time it was. "Look, Darling. The living room now has upholstered seats and cushions with zippers and corded edges that I am so proud of. Even the ottoman that came with the recliner looks brand new."

Pe kissed me on top of my head, "I am proud of you. Let's always keep this furniture in our home to remind us of where we are now and how far God is going to bring us."

Soon I was sewing drapes, and the little apartment looked warm and cozy.

Untold Treasures

I had still been budgeting five dollars a week on groceries for our family, and it was getting harder to stretch it.

One day, Pe came in from work and held up several tickets as the children and I rushed to greet him. "Guess what? I was given seven meal tickets to use at the hospital cafeteria. The human resource manager said I will get them every month." The children squealed with joy as they danced around their Phay Phay.

We did not have the money to buy even a glass of soda, let alone eat out, so visiting the hospital cafeteria became our special family treat. Every Sunday after church, we enjoyed lunch there, budgeting two tickets each week as Zaw and I shared our plates with Mimi. Pe was provided free meals at the hospital, so we were able to stretch this new luxury to four weeks each month.

It blew our minds how blessings were poured on us—unexpectedly and unsought. Pe came home one evening carrying a cardboard box. "Look what I've got in here!" Pulling out a color TV, he laughed. "My name was drawn at a medical meeting, and I'm probably the only doctor without a TV."

Just hearing the children holding hands and singing the song Pe had taught them, "God Is So Good," at the top of their voices was so beautiful.

One evening, Pe came home with a surprise announcement, "Dr. Arnold, my senior ophthalmologist, said he wants to pay Zaw's kindergarten tuition for one year so that we can send Zaw to a Christian school."

So many unexpected kindnesses. So much outpouring of love. We were overwhelmed. God provided miracle after miracle as He poured into our lives—treasures pressed down, shaken together, and running over.

The Richest Lady in Town

How was it that I was called "the richest lady in town," coined by a dear friend from the church we had started to attend? I never understood—because we certainly didn't have much. We still lived in our one-bedroom almost-windowless basement apartment, where neighborhood kids now loved to hang out.

We hosted walk-in backyard Bible studies, ladies' Bible fellowships, and small group get-togethers, and there were many times when people just dropped in with a plate of brownies or a home-baked apple pie. We felt such affection, warmth, and togetherness. Even with no possessions, we were loved and accepted.

One day, a neighbor came over with a package tied with a silver bow. "I thought of you when I saw this, and I just had to get it for you." I untied the bow, and tears filled my eyes as I saw beautiful stitching in an etched silver frame that reminded me of my mother's needlepoint treasures. On the camel-colored canvas, intricately cross stitched in gold thread, were the words, "The Love in our Home is a Gift from God. It is Given so we may Give it Away."

She hugged me. "You and your husband are always brimming over with love. It is a joy each time we walk into your home. I know my children adore the time that they spend here. Thank you for sharing your happiness."

Little Pete from the third-floor apartment would come over every day after school. He saw our children doing chores and wanted to do everything they did. He looked wistfully at the broom and dustpan in the hallway. "May I take this broom and sweep your floor clean? I want to help."

He was an only child and had a roomful of expensive toys, but the empty cardboard boxes that our children crafted things with were more appealing to him, and he loved sitting on the floor with Zaw and Mimi and listening to the Bible stories Melissa or I read to them.

His father, who had once told me he didn't believe in God, dropped in one day. "Do you mind if I come in? I want to see what has changed my son from acting like a spoiled child to being a very helpful and obedient kid."

He stayed awhile to listen as I finished reading the story of Daniel in the lion's den.

"Thank you, Mrs. Tin. I would love to come back with Pete to spend time here."

I never knew his motive for showing up every week, but Pete said his father stopped using swear words.

Late one evening, when the children were already in bed, Pe came home excited. "Darling, guess what happened today?" Lifting me off my feet and twirling me around and around, he blurted, "We get to stay in Chattanooga! Let's thank the Lord together first, and I will tell you all about it."

He sat me down, and as we held hands, he bowed his head. "Thank you, Jesus. You have promised in Your Word that You will be our provider, and You truly have been." He kissed my forehead.

"The Lord answered our prayers. They accepted me into the eye program." Pe, already an experienced surgeon back in Burma who had performed eye surgeries and given sight to his patients in those years, was now offered a place in the Chattanooga University of Tennessee three-year eye residency program, a sought-after appointment even for natural-born US citizens. God had poured out on us riches immeasurable.

Penned across my first Bible are these words poured out from my grateful heart:

> *I suffered extreme poverty, but He became my sufficiency. I suffered emptiness, but He became my friend, my companion. I suffered depression, but He became my joy, my hope, my light. In my weakness, He became my strength. He took my empty religion and gave me new life. He took me from my family and brought me into his family. He took away my material possessions and gave me Himself. He took away my restless, empty heart and gave me a new heart.*

And He began the process of pouring out His riches, treasures that will not rust or be corrupted, where thieves cannot break in and steal them. *I have loved you with an everlasting love, therefore with loving kindness have I drawn you*—and I will never, never, never let you go.

He is the "baying hound" in pursuit of those He has created for Himself. He is the "Lover of our soul" and waits with outstretched arms for us to come to Him and rest. I finally found rest in the only One who could fill that empty place in my heart with His peace.

"So," Melissa asked, already knowing what my answer would be, "Was it riches to rags or rags to riches?"

"For me, it is rags to riches and finally redemption! I had been searching for God with my whole heart, but it is He who has drawn me to Himself. I am still overwhelmed that my loving heavenly Father has transferred me from the domain of the darkness of my Buddhist heritage into the marvelous light of His Son."

I took her hand as we both teared up.

"Melissa, you have been instrumental in showing me the love of Jesus. You have been His hands and feet to our family."

So many treasures were to follow. My search for Him had ended, but a new chapter in my life was just beginning. He was putting me on a journey where He would continue writing my story until the last line in the final chapter is completed.

Chapter 34

My Cup Runneth Over

Give, and it will be given to you.
A good measure, pressed down,
shaken together, and running over,
will be poured into your lap.
For with the measure you use,
it will be measured to you.
–Luke 6:38 NIV

As soon as his rotating internship was over, Pe was admitted to the eye program at the Erlanger Hospital Campus. Because of his years of experience, he quickly took on leadership responsibilities and advanced his skills in eye surgery.

His attending physicians and medical director gave Pe recognition and personal attention and were very caring to him and our family. We were invited to their homes, and they made us feel very welcome. The medical director was the same generous man who had made sure our son could attend a Christian school by paying his tuition for a year.

Finally, the news came from Burma that Daddy and Mummy and my two younger sisters were able to immigrate to Australia. It was a relief that the

Burmese government had finally released them, although Esme had chosen to remain with her husband in Rangoon.

We were now settled in Chattanooga and had made many friends. Melissa still came over to do backyard Bible studies, and Zaw and Mimi were still in her Sunday School class. But we moved up from the basement to a ground-floor apartment.

"How's the sewing machine? Is it still working well for you?"

"Yes, it's holding up well. We also still have the old Ford Fairlane Pe bought for two hundred dollars. The radiator is no longer leaking, but the seats were ripped when we bought it and started to look terrible, so I made it a project. I found some vinyl and velvet—all the seats are now covered and look fresh and new, thanks to the sewing machine you gave me."

Melissa chuckled, "God knew what you needed. He just used me to deliver it."

That summer, we went down to Florida. It was so much fun to ride in our little car, remembering our early days when we had to walk everywhere.

We also took that little car to visit Pe's sister and her family in New York City for our annual Christmas trips. When we could not afford to stay at a motel, we would stop and sleep in the car for a few hours in the bitter cold and wake up with kinks in our necks, but it was worth it. Seeing the Rockefeller Center and the whole city lit up for the season's festivities was such a joyous time.

The mountains of Gatlinburg, Tennessee, were our go-to place, and the visitor's strip in Pigeon Forge was our favorite sightseeing area. On one trip there, another blessing came out of nowhere.

While Zaw and Mimi looked longingly at the posters at Silver Dollar City, now known as Dolly Parton's "Dollywood," a man approached Pe and offered him four tickets. Thinking he would have to buy the tickets, which was nowhere in our budget, Pe smiled and shook his head. "No, take them. I'm giving them to you," the man said. "We're going to leave and can't use them, and I want your family to enjoy the show." How grateful we were, and what a beautiful way for the children to see the endless joy sharing can bring.

A Golden Summer

We will always remember that first year of Pe's residency when he was offered training at Colby College and our entire family was transferred to Maine for the summer. We drove in our little Ford Fairlane up to the tiny cottage the college rented for us.

"It's right on the lake, Darling! It looks so peaceful."

Zaw was jumping up and down, "Look, Phay Phay! There is a boat as well." And indeed, a tiny, non-motorized boat, which we could use throughout the summer evenings, was tied up at a small dock.

"Look, May May!" Mimi exclaimed. "There are two bedrooms. I can put my teddy bear in one of them." Each bedroom was only the size of a full-size bed, and to get into the rooms, we literally had to climb onto the bed.

A tiny stall shower was adjacent to a tiny closet-like bathroom. "We can hang our clothes in the hall closet, and there's a mirror on the door."

"Look at this narrow room. It looks like a galley on a ship." There was a small, combined kitchen and dining area where we cooked, ate, talked, and had a wonderful, carefree time. We would wash our clothes in the tiny sink and then lay them out to dry on the nearby bushes.

It was a summer to remember. At the end of it, we drove home refreshed and renewed, thanking God for His goodness to us.

With Pe's eye residency came more regular hours. Unless Pe was on call and had to stay overnight at the hospital, he worked an eight-hour shift and had time to bond with the children and play tennis each week. He and Zaw would make paper airplanes and boats. "Phay Phay, let's build a radio-controlled boat and an airplane one day."

Pe promised and kept his promise. Together, they built several planes and a helicopter and a sophisticated boat to which they attached a radio control mechanism.

With Mimi, Pe would find time to play dolls and build paper houses. And she loved opening an imaginary restaurant or performing a pretend pantomime play with him.

As Zaw got older, Pe taught him carpentry skills while he took care of the plumbing and repairs, fixing everything that needed maintenance as we could not afford outside help.

A Six-Love, Six-Love Score

"I have found a tennis partner who can play with me once a week." During his internship year, Pe had to give up his favorite sport. I was so happy when he had time to play again. On Monday evenings after work, he went to the Manker Patten clay courts to meet his singles partner and play the game he loved so much.

He took part in several tournaments, and at one spectacular tournament, I was at the edge of my seat, watching him play as he finished off the singles game 6-0, 6-0, winning the competition. I marveled at the ease with which he swung the racket and his comfortable stance as he hit the tennis ball from side to side across the net, letting the ball bounce just inside the boundary lines of the court as his opponent scrambled from one end of the sidelines to the other.

He was cool as a cucumber, while the young man on the opposite side of the court seemed hot and agitated, finally throwing down his racket as he lost. Pe went and shook his hand. "You played a good game. Your forearm swings were great. You look so young to be over thirty-five." With hilarity, we realized they had entered Pe, who was nearly forty, in a twenty- to twenty-five-year-old singles slot.

Another Move

In Pe's final year of residency, we moved from our tiny apartment to a home that would have been beyond our means to purchase except that God provided. Initially, we did not have much left over after paying the mortgage, but it gradually got easier. Our home became a special place of hospitality as we opened our doors wide to friends who had become very dear to us as well as to all new friends.

"I love that our house is a haven for our children and all their friends from school and church."

"Yes, and I am so glad we can have Sunday School parties and cozy dinners with friends on our backyard deck. I am glad we have a bigger house so we can host dinners and prepare meals for people who blessed us when we had nothing."

We never forgot the kindness of the ophthalmologist who had paid for Zaw's kindergarten tuition. We began a "Gratitude Return"—each year helping a different child attend a Christian school for a new school year.

Pe loved his three years of eye residency. "I enjoy the skills training I receive every year and the opportunity to attend the National Eye Academy Conferences. I will take the board exam in three months and graduate at the end of this month, but I am going to volunteer my time to teach surgery to all the eye residents who come through this program in Chattanooga."

"Darling, I am so proud of you. You are an excellent teacher and are already training the younger residents."

"I would also like to attend other conferences, especially the American Society of Cataract and Refractive Surgeons Symposiums. They have excellent courses for Practice Administrators, and we can both learn up-to-date management and procedures."

We began attending these yearly symposiums together to keep up with the latest innovations in the ophthalmic field. Even today, after more than forty years as a Certified Ophthalmic Executive and Administrator, I continue to learn and grow.

Because of Your Ethnic Background

Once his residency was completed and he passed the boards, Pe was ready to see patients. However, the senior ophthalmologist he was looking to work for did not feel he would be right for his practice because of his ethnic background.

"I am so sorry, Dr. Tin. You are an excellent physician and surgeon, but I don't think you will be a good fit for my practice." This was the year

1978, and we were a very tiny minority in a predominantly white Southern community, but Pe was undeterred.

He began work as a part-time surgical assistant at Memorial Hospital and assisted in all types of surgeries, including heart, orthopedic, and head surgery. The best part of this was that the long afternoons were ours, and we enjoyed our time together as we rested, worked, and planned for our future practice, which we trusted the Lord would provide in His perfect timing.

Then God opened an amazing door. Pe was invited by a senior ophthalmologist, who had also been one of his attending professors, to work half days at his busy practice.

"Hey, Dr. Tin, I've watched you with the patients when you were in the residency program. You have a special bedside manner and are skilled in what you do. I'm getting very busy, and it would help me if you could work for me as soon as possible."

"I'd love to, sir. When do you want me to start?"

"The beginning of next week is fine. Just show up at the office, and my practice manager will take good care of you. She knows you already. She said you did cataract surgery on her father's eyes and that he is so pleased he doesn't need to wear glasses anymore."

Pe took the offer, turned in his resignation as a part-time surgical assistant, and was overjoyed to use his skills for eye patients. The patients loved his caring, gentle manner, and with his senior ophthalmologist's blessing, they followed him to our new practice when we opened our doors.

God not only provided for our needs, but He poured out on us immeasurable riches. He fills up our cups daily, pressed down, shaken together, and overflowing. He has given us more than we can hold on to, and with wide-open hands, we gratefully accept them as grace gifts to grace others with His love.

Chapter 35

God's Preparation and Provision

For we are his workmanship,
created in Christ Jesus unto good works,
which God hath before ordained
that we should walk in them.
–Ephesians 2:10 KJV

Kind hearts are the gardens, Kind thoughts are the roots,
Kind words are the blossoms, Kind deeds are the fruits.
–Henry Wadsworth Longfellow[1]

Soon, we launched out as pioneers and opened our own solo ophthalmology practice. Pe was excited. "We can rent an office from another ophthalmologist. She has built a multi-specialty building that can house at least four practices and offered me a space."

"We can take out a small business loan of $47,000 with a term of seven years to furnish one of the two examining rooms, a business office, and a small waiting room, leaving enough money for rent, utilities, and supplies." My business mind went into motion. "Let's leave the other examining room as an empty space where Mimi and Zaw can do their homework and play after I pick them up from school."

We knew that one exam room was all we would need as we did not yet have a patient following. The children did not have much to play with. But, as in our previous basement apartment, they built up their skills of design and invention as they used empty cardboard boxes to create spaces. Years later, Mimi, who became a flourishing graphic designer in many different venues, said of the forced creativity in that extra office space, "This is where I got my creative juices flowing."

We began with a start-up solo clinic, waiting for patients to show up. I handled the business office duties with the help of a friend who worked for us without pay. Linda and her husband were instrumental in the implementation of our new venture. Not only did she help us daily during our initial year, but Curtis also assisted us in applying for the Small Business Administration loan, and when we changed our office to computer-based, he set it up for us.

"We can't afford help yet, Darling, so if you'll mow the grass, I can clean the bathrooms and the entire clinic between my medical work."

Days would go by as we waited for patients to come, but Pe was not worried. "God will multiply. We must simply keep on being faithful with what little we have."

When the first patients walked through the door, we were so excited. And slowly, our practice base grew and multiplied. Pe said, "Let's open early and stay late. And if we work on snow days, some patients needing emergency eyecare might show up."

Patients who could not get an appointment with their eye doctors would call us; we were always thankful and took care of them with grateful hearts. And although no general practitioners gave us referrals because they already had their own ophthalmologists to refer their eye patients to, we began to get referrals from patients who had come to see us.

Each night we would hold hands and thank the Lord for His provision, and Pe would always end the prayer, saying, "Jesus, You are our Shepherd. We will not want for anything because You are our Provider and the Giver of all good things. We love You, and we trust You. In Your name, we pray."

Each morning I would pray, "Dear Jesus, guide Pe's hands, his mind, and his eyes. And fill him with all that You are so that out of him will flow rivers of living water that will touch and heal people's lives."

Our mission, even from the very beginning, has always been "Caring for your vision. Caring for you." And the patients we saw could see and feel our love and care for them. To this day, they continue to refer their friends and family to us.

As we worked hard to grow our practice, God poured out His infinite provision on my husband's calling as a healer of sight. Loved and respected by so many of his peers, my kind and gentle Pe became a leading eye surgeon. He was well-known in his field as an innovator and was at the forefront in the latest technology to improve vision correction.

A February Miracle

Three years into our practice, we sat down and looked at our budget. I ventured, "I think the rent is too high, Darling. Let's look for a place that we can buy and own."

Pe agreed, and after looking at a few places, the Lord led us to a beautiful three-story Victorian home built in 1903, resplendent with seven fireplaces, twelve-foot ceilings, oak flooring, an elegant staircase, and huge pocket doors. Listed on the National Gallery of Historic Homes, it sat right at the busy crossroads of Third and Central Avenue.

"Let's use the parlor as an optical boutique. The family rooms on the main floor can be our two exam rooms. And I can use the dining room as our business office."

Pe added, "This huge kitchen can be divided into two more examination rooms."

It was the month of February when we turned in our one-month notice for the office space we had been renting. We moved out exactly twenty-eight days after purchasing the house, so that the rent and mortgage would only overlap for one month—because that was all we could afford.

We also could not afford to hire a remodeling company. So after seeing patients, we would go to the house to strip wallpaper, paint, sand the wooden floors, install ceilings and safety bars, and do all the repairs that needed to be done. We worked hard the entire month of February.

Our friend Wanda talked to us after church. "Hey, Nita, Boyd and I can help you. It's too much to do by yourselves. I'll come bright and early every day, and Boyd can come after work."

Another couple, whose teenage son Pe had treated, showed up to help. Ruby said, "Steve can drywall, put up new ceilings, paint, and hang decorative safety iron bars in every window, and I can scrape wallpaper and help in any way."

I felt a lump in my throat. "You are beyond kind. We do need to finish by the end of the month and will be so grateful for your help."

Steve nodded. "My dad said he can whittle replacement spindles for your beautiful tiger oak staircase, and my mom said she will sew the drapes for those high windows."

These dear people, who became our closest friends, showed up every day of the week and worked tirelessly alongside us. We scraped, stripped, hammered, nailed, tacked, glued, shined, and polished as, each day, the beauty of the place unfolded before our eyes.

We were still seeing patients the entire month of February at the rental building. At the end of each day, we would leave the office and go to work on the house, just a few blocks away, letting our children sleep on the sofa in the unused exam room until we returned.

Once, Steve kept working with us almost halfway into the night. I didn't realize the time had melted away until Pe wearily said, "If we put away everything, we can go back to the office and shower there just in time for you to take the kids to school. I'll open the office because the patients will be showing up."

"What time is it?" I yawned.

"Six-thirty. The sun is just coming up. Let's hurry!"

I thought of the pediatrician who had come by at the beginning of our project, marveled at the scope of our work, and said, "It will be a miracle if you complete it by the end of February."

And it was. We persevered, our sweet friends gave 100 percent, and the Lord was with us. On February 28, 1981, we dedicated our Oak Street Office to the Lord, giving it to Him with open hands. And on March 1, we saw our first patients at the new location.

Touching Lives

The atmosphere we created continues to this day. It is homey and relaxing, and patients enjoy the ambiance. True to our mission statement, each person is treated as our guest and loves that they are cared for as if they were family. This beautiful building is still our flagship office, and we try to maintain its originality. It has seen many changes and renovations with the passing of time, but it still serves us faithfully.

Pe's practice grew rapidly, but he still gave a huge portion of his time to the community. From the time he finished his residency and opened his own practice, he became the designated Surgical Skills Instructor for all the eye residents rotating through the University of Tennessee Eye Program in Chattanooga.

To this program, Pe gave twenty-seven years as a voluntary professor, teaching and helping young eye doctors learn ophthalmic surgical skills, even while building and maintaining his solo practice. For almost three decades, Pe donated over seven to eight hours of his time every week. Not only did he teach surgery skills to the eye residents each Monday, but he also assisted them in major eye surgeries on Wednesdays and, later, assisted them in LASIK surgeries on Fridays.

"Darling," Pe said one day, "The Willie D. Miller Eye Center at the Erlanger Health Systems will soon open. The eye residents will be trained with top-of-the-line laser equipment." It became a very busy place and was utilized by almost all the ophthalmologists.

The Miller Eye Center was managed by the senior ophthalmologists who gave their time and money until they passed, then another administration took over. Although Pe was taken for granted by the person in charge of the eye program, he continued to serve faithfully for many years as the leading surgical skills volunteer professor.

This was his work, his ministry, his joy, but the many hours left him little time to concentrate on his own practice. So he eventually reluctantly resigned and left this teaching position.

He was formally invited back as a salaried professor because he was valued for his finesse in surgery skills, but he declined because we had now opened a satellite practice in Georgia. The eye program closed soon after.

From a bare-bones, tiny clinic, waiting for patients to show up to a thriving practice where patients were waiting to see him, God poured out His infinite provision on Pe's calling as a healer of sight. Loved and respected by his peers, my kind and gentle husband became one of the leading eye surgeons in our part of the country.

Recognizing his surgical skills, Pe was given the honor of taking part in the research for the introduction of the LASIK procedure into North America under FDA approval. He was also chosen as one of the investigators for the procedure for implantation of the posterior lens following cataract surgery and was one of the first surgeons to introduce the small incision, sutureless lens removal.

He would tell me, "Everything I have is because God has provided. He gave me you, and you have always been by my side." Pe always gives God the glory as he gratefully acknowledges Proverbs 16:9, one of his favorite passages: "In their hearts humans plan their course, but the LORD establishes their steps" (NIV).

We began to understand that God had wanted Pe to start his own practice for our good and His glory, not ours. Our disappointment in being rejected because of his ethnicity was truly God's appointment. God was going to use us in ways we could not even imagine.

And God has truly orchestrated Pe's life and abundantly blessed his faithfulness. To this day, he is well known in his field as an innovator and is forefront in the latest technology to improve vision correction. Patients love him dearly as he continues caring for them as though they were his own. And as he prays for them before and after surgery. After more than forty years of Pe's being in practice, God still uses him to touch the lives of those who come to him for treatment.

Chapter 36

The American Dream

Who dreamt a dream so strong, so brave, so true,
That even yet its mighty daring sings.
In every brick and stone, in every furrow turned.
That's made America the land it has become.
O, I'm the man who sailed those early seas.
–Langston Hughes[1]

As it is written: "What no eye has seen,
what no ear has heard,
and what no human mind has conceived"—
the things God has prepared for those who love him.
–1 Corinthians 2:9 NIV

In 1982, we were unexpectedly given the opportunity to purchase a house on a lake. This was an amazing provision from God, as the owner and builder sold it to us for what it cost him, although comparable lake homes cost three-and-a-half times more. By the time we bought the house, we were no longer struggling, but we were still on a tight budget and living within our means.

Our dear friend Melissa graduated from Tennessee Temple University and moved back to Ohio, her home state, but she kept in touch. We had to tell her more of what God did.

"Melissa, I cannot believe all we have been blessed with. Can you imagine? You were with us from the beginning—so you know how unreal this all is. I mean, from the twenty dollars we had when we first came to the US to riches overflowing, from being cooped up in a one-bedroom basement apartment to owning a breathtaking home. Our gratitude is unending. From having to walk because we didn't own a car to being able to travel for over twenty years on mission trips, evangelizing, encouraging, and providing general medical and eye treatment and surgeries, our hearts are full to overflowing."

My heart was bursting as I continued to tell Melissa all that had been happening for us.

"From receiving an unsought year of tuition for our son's kindergarten at a church school to being able to sponsor a deserving child annually to attend a Christian school has brought us deep fulfillment and unexplainable joy. And you. You reached out to us and have been such a treasure."

God not only provided for our needs, but He has also poured out riches full to overflowing on us. Even to this day, as our children and grandchildren flourish and grow.

Living the Dream

We worked hard and saved for our children's schooling but also gave away what the Lord laid upon our hearts. Everything God supplied was ours with an open hand to share with others, and the more we gave, the more it was multiplied. This was true riches, and what joy it gave us because, as Pe would say, "Riches are given to us by our heavenly Father so that we might give them away to bless others and bring Him glory."

We caught the attention of an editor of a local magazine. Under the title, "A Chattanoogan Family Lives the American Dream," she interviewed us and wrote,

I was granted an interview with Pe Than Tin, MD, FACS, a well-known eye surgeon, and his wife, Nita. I visited their amazing lake home, which was three stories high, with a swimming pool and boat house, expansive grounds where their daughter Mimi Tin, an up-and-coming graphic designer had created an exotic Japanese garden, complete with a gazebo, a bridge over a curving stream and a waterfall that cascaded from natural-looking rocks. Their son, Zaw, is currently an internal medicine specialist at the Cleveland Hospital, and his wife is in family practice.

When asked about the history behind the outdoor spaces and the beautiful gardens, Nita, with her slight British accent said, "We planned this because it reminds us of the luxury of our country home in Burma. With our love for gardens, we slowly added a rose garden, two water lily ponds, a lotus pool with a tinkling waterfall, enchanted and secret hideaways, an English garden abloom with roses, hydrangeas and phlox and camellias, and a flagstone-paved outdoor dining area where we have comfy chairs covered with floral cushions that remind us of England."

She paused and smiled, "Nostalgic afternoons spent having tea either in the English garden or out on the circular patio facing the lake and then having dinner in the gazebo in the enchanted garden is a pleasurable experience for many of our guests. My husband has a green thumb, loves gardening, and does all the work himself."

My next question was addressed to the handsome Dr. Tin. "Your house is right on the lake. I noticed you have a ski boat and a couple of jet skis. Do you enjoy being out on the lake?"

"Oh yes!" he said. "We have pool and ski parties every year for more than sixty-five church youth and kids. Their teachers and pastors bring their boats, and they all love hanging out here. A lot of food, fun and fellowship, followed by music, a message, and prayer time."

"We also host Sunday school parties, Christmas dinners, Bible studies, ladies' retreats, cookouts, and barbeques. We have our annual fish fry and Christmas in July for our pastors and their families, and we make full use of our jet skis and Sea-doos and ski-boat."

"What is this Christmas in July, Dr. Tin?"

"We do this annually, and it is a time when we honor all our pastors, church staff and their families. It is a time of gift-giving from us, as well as a ski-swim-barbeque fellowship retreat for them."

"I have heard also that you go on several mission trips each year and that you perform surgeries on school benches and on church pews. I'd love to hear about it."

"Well, the Lord has opened up so many opportunities. For about seven years we have traveled with the medical-dental team with our church to small remote villages way up in the mountains in Honduras where there are no clinics or hospitals. It is a two-and-a-half-day journey, and in the three days that we have a clinic next to our preaching tent, we treat over several thousand people who have walked long distances. I perform about thirty eye surgeries a day and have done cataract surgeries with intraocular implants, and a few muscle surgeries to correct crossed eyes, using only numbing eye drops."

Nita added, "My husband has also traveled to Venezuela with a team, and I have accompanied him on several trips to Malta with our church. It has been an amazing experience to share God's love with them as we take care of their needs, whether it is at home, at our work, or in a different country."

My curiosity was aroused, "What is the heartbeat behind all of this?"

"We have been given much, and it is our hearts' desire to serve and to share. We wouldn't have it otherwise."

Their hospitality and grace shone. I left their home where I had truly felt the peace of God. This was a family who was truly living the American Dream, not because of the things they own but because of the things they could share.[2]

What I didn't know then as we said goodbye to the charming editor was that the Lord was not only going to pour His blessings on us and use us as a funnel to bless others, but that He was also in the process of refining me so that my testimony would make known to many the riches of His glory.

Life for me now took a different turn.

Part V

My Soul's Desire

Chapter 37

Life on a Merry-Go-Round

"Come to me, all you who are weary and burdened,
and I will give you rest.
Take my yoke upon you and learn from me,
for I am gentle and humble in heart,
and you will find rest for your souls.
For my yoke is easy and my burden is light."
–Matthew 11:28–30 NIV

With growth comes challenges and more responsibilities. Without realizing it, my life began moving at a faster pace than I wanted it to go. Our practice was dedicated to God's service, and He was always the center of it, as He was our home. And God provided and allowed the practice to grow into one of excellence.

We had struggled for many years, but the foundation was built solidly on God's principles, and despite the competition around us, we not only survived but thrived.

Compassionate care and competency were always the core values we offered to all our patients. After forty years, those values remained central to our practice—patients could talk to or pray with the surgeon and physician who cared for them.

My studies in biology, mathematics, strategic planning, English literature, and language became useful. I was the CEO, the CFO, and the COO. And I took care of clinical issues, human resources, payroll, strategic planning, legal and government issues, chart dictations, audits, coding, insurance contract negotiations, credentialing, accounting, payables, receivables, and corporate taxes. And although I gradually delegated much of the work, the many years of constant overload eventually took their toll.

Pe was a healer and not interested in administrative work. So, I took over every department, both medical and business, and I worked long hours. He tried to help me, but sitting at a desk and poring over figures was not his forte.

Once, when I had been going over some accounting books with him, he fell asleep. "Your eyes are closed, Darling. I know these spreadsheets bore you, but don't you want to know how we are doing?"

"Not really. I just like doing surgery and seeing patients. And you like statistics and do such a wonderful job taking care of our practice. I think I'll go and make some hot cocoa. Would you like some?"

I had to chuckle. Pe loved cooking and grocery shopping and spent hours concocting gourmet meals, all artistically presented. And he would call up to my office with, "Dinner is ready, Darling." At the end of the meal, he would always say, "Thank you, Darling."

What more could I ask for?

Pe always looked forward to mealtimes and the preparations. Even after a long day of surgery, cooking was never a chore for him. He delighted in surprising me with an array of mouthwatering dishes.

Living with Pe was life on a different plane. He was full of joy and humor. There was always something to smile about, even when I was tired and impatient. He would always find a way for us to end up in a heap of laughter over something funny he said. My weariness over the day's heavy responsibilities would slide off like water as we giggled like two teenagers. Who could hold on to any drama when he made everything seem so light?

We had cozy, wonderful, intimate evenings. We would sit on the sofa near the fireplace and cuddle before we went to bed.

This was my husband, a beautiful, caring, and gifted man who gave himself unselfishly and loved me as Christ loved the church. This love also reached out to his patients, our employees, extended families, friends, and anyone the Lord brought into his life. He was generous to a fault. He loved well. At work, Pe prayed with and for his patients. And they looked forward to their visits with him. Our employees adored him, and our practice became a mission field.

Entering a Life of Busyness

Then began my speaking engagements. I was introduced in business circles as a special event speaker:

> *Nita Tin is a certified ophthalmic executive and is the administrator and co-founder of her husband's ophthalmology practice, Tin Laser Vision Center, which they founded single-handedly in 1978 in Chattanooga, Tennessee. Their practice is in the historic Fort Wood area, and it has become the flagship office for the* Tin Laser Vision & The Aesthetic and Wellness Medical Spa.

*In 1990 they opened another location in Fort Oglethorpe,
Georgia. She has served many years in her capacity as an administrator and chief operating and financial officer, and she
is the secretary for Dr. Tin's professional corporation.*

I was faithful in my roles as a wife and the mother of our two children—both of whom accepted the Lord early in their childhood, excelled
in their work, became responsible young adults, and made our lives as
parents very easy.

Pe and I were a team, and we worked, lived, and laughed together, enjoying
each other's company. He would chuckle and say, "We are two peas in a
pod."

I would hug him and whisper, "We are soulmates and always will be."

Our lives were centered around our home, church, school, and work. And
I learned to juggle all this, including attending weekly Bible studies at
Precept Ministries International, teaching Sunday school, and serving in
the Training Union at my church.

When I look back, however, I wish I had learned to say *no*. Everything I
did was innately good, but I had no discernment at that stage to choose
between the good and the best, and I was sucked into the world's mold
of staying constantly busy instead of walking God's specific path for me. I
was building my own story instead of joining God's story.

I became an active member on the prayer committee, the personnel committee, the ladies' ministry committee, the family ministry committee, and
later took on the teaching for the weekly ladies' Bible studies, where I
taught faithfully for twenty-five years.

I was doing the Lord's work, or so it seemed. I was doing good work at our business, at home, and in ministry. But I was struggling to balance all three areas. How could I have known that time was precious and that my leftovers would never be enough for what God had planned for me?

My unusual testimony drew interest. I was presented as a woman who had been rescued from fear and tyranny and delivered to freedom and faith.

From 1974 to the present, Mrs. Nita Tin, formerly a Buddhist, has spoken at several venues. She has been invited to local churches, including several churches around the nation and internationally—in Sydney, Australia, and Malta. She has spoken at business and civic clubs, public schools, and private Christian schools.

While a guest of Dr. James Dobson, she was asked to speak at a Focus on the Family gathering at the Alisal Ranch and was the lead speaker for the National Young Women's Conference in Chattanooga. She has led many women's retreats and prayer circles and is a frequent speaker at the Scenic City Women's Network for Christian Businesswomen.

She was invited by Precept International to share her testimony in interviews with Kay Arthur, which aired on a national broadcast and was briefly mentioned on the Moody Bible broadcast In the Market with Janet Parshall.

She has written several short articles and has a section, Nita's Nook, in the Grace Sunday School Class Newsletter and in the Bayside Church Ladies Newsletter. She has contributed several devotionals to The Promises of God, a book published by the Scenic City Women's Network.

God had placed in my mouth a new song, but where I had previously poured over God's Word and spent extended time alone in prayer with the Lord, I now barely had enough time even to process my day-to-day activities and responsibilities. Although knowing Him more was my heart's desire, my time spent in His Word, except for my Bible studies and preparation, grew less and less.

I was on a merry-go-round. Joy seemed elusive, and life was an endless seesaw of worry, stress, exhaustion, and mental turmoil. I longed to go back to where I had been, but the urgency of the moment always seemed to rear its ugly head as I put out one fire after the other.

I confided in Pe. "At times, I feel as though I just need to take in a long breath of air and fill my lungs."

He held me close and smoothed my furrowed brow, "The battle is not yours, Darling. The Lord has already gone before you and will always fight your battles for you. Jesus is asking you to come to Him. He will give you rest."

At those times, the Lord met me right where I was.

Just as Moses cried out, "LORD, show me Your glory!" when he met with God in the mountain, and God hid him in the cleft of the rock, it was also my heart's cry. "Hide me, dear Lord" was my constant prayer, and God, my Jehovah *Shammah,* hid me in the secret depths of His tent, holding me close until the storms that seemed to threaten passed by.

All during this time, God kept reminding me of the book He had called me to write to tell others the story He Himself had written in my life. He reminded me repeatedly that He had lifted me out of a horrible pit, out of the miry clay, and that He had not only established the path for me but had also put a new song in my mouth so that others would put their trust in Him.

Obedience to His calling was what God was looking for. I knew in my heart what God wanted, but writing my story was always put off because there were a thousand-and-one things I needed to take care of first. I had so many excuses to offer God. Yet because I was neither hot nor cold, I secretly wondered if God would take away my new song.

My heart longed for that first intimacy, that sacred time when I would put aside everything and spend time with Him in the garden of His heart. At times like these, which were getting fewer and farther apart, my heart's longing would drive me to my knees. And God would meet me every time.

However, life continued year after year. It seemed there was no way of getting off the merry-go-round. It was not until depths of sorrow upon sorrow came in waves that my anguished heart finally realized this was not life abundant, and it was not what my heavenly Father wanted for me. Jesus had come that my joy would be full, but I was at rock bottom. On the outside, I ministered, worked, and strived to be all things to all people. But inside, I found no rest.

Chapter 38

The Master Potter

Yet you, LORD, are our Father.
We are the clay, you are the potter;
we are all the work of your hand.
–Isaiah 64:8 NIV

Year 2000 came. My life was still spinning out of control. In the back of my mind, I still had the sense that something always needed to be done. God's call to write my book was still on my list, but it was not in the urgent pile.

Then my world—our world—changed. In early October, we heard the dreaded word *cancer*. "Dr. Tin, I have the results from your biopsy," his surgeon said with compassion. "You have prostate cancer. At this moment, it is 40 percent contained. We need to take care of it immediately. You will have some choices to make."

I sat on the small chair in the corner of the examination room, stunned. *What about the 60 percent that is not contained?* my heart whispered, beating frantically.

As though I was listening from the opposite end of a long tunnel, I heard Pe say in his gentle, quiet voice. "The Lord is in control."

And the surgeon replied, "That is good to hear, Dr. Tin. I will be praying for you."

Pe did not say that from a Calvinist or any other theological persuasion. It wasn't that at all. With a decidedly pure and simple faith, he trusted his life completely in the hands of his loving heavenly Father. That's who he was.

Holding hands tightly, we got back to our car. Pe had ten surgical cases waiting for him at the hospital, and I was going to drop him off and go on to my Wednesday Bible Study class at our church, where I was teaching. On the way, Pe quoted Psalm 91 in its entirety.

What an amazing God! He had impressed upon Pe's heart to memorize this psalm months before this happened. "Darling," he said, "God knew we would need to rest on His promises contained in Psalm 91."

"What is amazing to me is that you can never remember a poem or song, but the Lord has this whole psalm imprinted on your heart!"

I dropped Pe off at the hospital. His sweet smile was imprinted on my own heart. *He is the heart of my heart. I cannot bear to lose him.* My mind drummed this message repeatedly as I drove to the church.

Many of the ladies there were his patients. I would have to tell them, but I could also tell them that he had told his surgeon that God was in control, and it would be an encouragement to them as a few of them were going through rough patches in their own lives. *Was that what I needed to tell my heart also?*

What amazed me more was that my husband accepted all this as from his loving Father's hand. It was as though he just sat in his Father's lap and said, *You made me; I know You will take care of me,* and then slept through each night as though he were a baby.

As for me, I would lie awake, and when I became too restless and did not want to wake Pe up, I would go to my home office across the hall and sing, "I must tell Jesus, I must tell Jesus, I cannot bear these burdens alone. In my distress, He surely will help me. I must tell Jesus; He ever lives to care for His own."[1]

Cancer! I never thought it would come home to stay with us. I thought of my first face-to-face encounter with cancer. Lisa, a young wife and mother I had taught in Sunday school, had been stricken with breast cancer. She had bravely gone through all the chemotherapy treatments. Still, the day she came to be checked out by my husband because she saw a dark spot, I held her sobbing body close as Pe told her the cancer had already spread and she needed to have laser treatment by a retina specialist. I drove her to that office and stayed with her during the treatment while her husband rushed over to be with her.

On the Sunday before she died, Pe, Mimi, and I dropped in to see her. Her husband was playing the piano, which he said seemed to help her. We kissed her and told her we loved her. Her mother was sitting on the other side of her bed, and as I went over to speak to her mother, Lisa beckoned me to come close to her.

She gripped my hand, and I held her hand in mine, softly quoting Psalm 23 and then saying, "Goodbye, sweetheart, Jesus is waiting for you. I will see you soon." She smiled and closed her eyes. That night, she passed through death to new life as she lay in her husband's arms.

As my mind returned to Lisa's journey home to meet her Savior, my heart was smitten within me. Would Pe be taken from me? I prayed silently, *Lord Jesus, look after him.*

The two-week wait before the scheduled surgery date seemed endless. Meanwhile, we traveled to Grier, South Carolina, to see our son, Zaw, and his wife, Sophia. Mimi traveled up from Atlanta to meet us at their house.

We held hands in a circle, and before Pe prayed, he said quietly, "I have cancer, but the Lord is going to take care of me." He again quoted Psalm 91.

As Mimi broke down and ran out of the room to cry in the bathroom, Sophia said to her, "We are in this together." And at that moment, God gave me these tender last verses in this Psalm, which I shared with all of them.

"Because he has loved Me, I will save him; I will set him securely on high, because he has known My name. He will call upon Me, and I will answer him; I will be with him in trouble; I will rescue him and honor him. I will satisfy him with a long life, And show him My salvation" (Psalm 91:14–16 NASB).

The weekend before the surgery, we went to our retreat. On our twenty-fifth anniversary, we had bought a chalet in Gatlinburg to which we had returned again and again, and we needed the quiet beauty of the mountains and the soothing serenity of our home atop the brow that overlooked Mt. LeConte. That last night, we sat hand in hand with no need for words as we watched the swirling mist frolicking in the gusty winds before slowly drifting up to the tops of the mountains. *Show me Thy glory, Lord*, I prayed as we sat there in the silence of the night, holding each other close.

Before we left Gatlinburg, we stopped at a little white church, knelt at the altar together, and lifted our hearts in full surrender to God.

With the radical prostatectomy surgery over, the surgeon came into the recovery room and pronounced with a lilt in his voice, "With cancer, you never say it is gone, but in your husband's case, we got it all, and the cancer is gone."

My heart leaped! Full of gratitude, I thanked the doctor. And over and over, I told the Lord, "You took care of him. You protected him as You said You would."

God was in control. Pe had taken God at His word. And the outcome was amazing.

Happy Birthday, Darling

Pe was released from the hospital on October 16, 2000. It was his sixtieth birthday. We arrived home to a surprise party. Both Mimi and Zaw had come for the celebration.

As Pe opened their presents, I realized I had nothing to give him. I quickly ran up to my office, and within ten minutes, the Lord gave me a poem. I printed it out from my computer, rolled it up neatly, and tied it with a red ribbon.

Pe untied the ribbon, unrolled the three pages of typed parchment sheets, and read,

> *Darling heart, I was barely sixteen and you were not yet twenty when God brought you into my life and changed me forever. We were both so shy, yet something bigger than ourselves drew us to each other, and we have never let go.*

> *God, in His love, bound us together so totally in His embrace*

and has tied us so intricately together. A love that God ignited, allowing the fire of our love to burn brightly for Him and for each other.

We are bound for eternity, Darling, and hand in hand, I press on life's journey with you. So different, yet in our sameness of soul and spirit and mind, we have pooled our life until the boundaries of two different lives enmesh and swirl together, forming one complete whole.

My soul mate, the one whom our Lord gifted me with, you alone have lifted me into the embrace of our triune God until we both stand before our Master, clothed in His righteousness and grace.

Love of my life, through your life I understood, your Maker became my Maker, your God became my God as hands out-stretched, I took the gift of pardon, so freely offered without ties. Unspeakable joy as you introduced me to your Savior, and He became my Savior too. One faith, one love, one hope, one joy—no longer separated, we became one in His love.

Precious children, gifts of heaven, Zaw and Mimi made our joy complete and full—as nourishing, strengthening, loving, guiding, learning, laughing, loving, growing—bathed in un-conditional love, our hearth and home became for us our haven of rest and refreshing full to overflowing as they too reached out for the gift of life, and warmed the depths of our being.

Hopes and dreams, shared and given, some to cherish, some to hold. Darling, we'll just keep on trekking till one day we reach our heavenly home. Hopes for our children and grandchildren, given into our Father's hands, knowing that He loves them completely, wanting what is best for them.

You and I have traveled this earthly road, clinging to each other, undergirded by our Father's strength, working through our joys and sorrows, furnished through the tapestry of His all-wise, never-ending love. Filled with questions, yet we've rested, faces upturned, hearts trusting in His unfailing merciful love.

We have found Him true and faithful as He promised in His Word. Darling heart, I almost lost you as this birthday came around. But our loving, heavenly Father glorified Himself in you, brought you through the storm, the raging tempest, when together we put our life, our hands, safe in His eternal love.

I thank you, Darling, for your love, your life, your sweetness, and your gentleness. You have made me a better person, and I cherish you with all my heart.

Tears rolled down his cheeks even as they did on mine. The children, too, were thankful that we all still had each other.

Chapter 39

The Refiner's Fire

For you, God, tested us; you refined us like silver.
You brought us into prison and laid burdens on our backs.
You let people ride over our heads;
we went through fire and water,
but you brought us to a place of abundance.
–Psalm 66:10-12 NIV

These have come so that the proven genuineness of your faith—of greater
worth than gold, which perishes even though refined by fire—may result
in praise, glory and honor when Jesus Christ is revealed.
–1 Peter 1:7 NIV

I was in the surgical waiting room while Pe was having his cancer surgery when my cell phone rang. It was my sister Gail in Australia. "Mummy is hospitalized. She is in a semi-coma. I know you cannot come to be with her, but I know you will be praying for her."

My heart was torn. They lived across a continent and an ocean, so far away. I wanted to be with her, but I could not leave Pe.

A week after Pe was discharged, I had an urgent call from my sister Chicky. "Tita, Gail's aorta has split all the way to her kidneys, and she is not expected to live."

This time I rushed across the continent and the ocean and was in time to see her in the intensive care unit at a Sydney hospital. She was unconscious and not expected to get through the night.

Travel weary after having taken four different airlines to get there as quickly as possible, I sat beside her all night, watching her vitals go off the chart.

I repeated Psalm 91 over and over and prayed aloud for her. "Lord Jesus, please don't let Gail die without knowing You."

Morning came, along with emergency surgery to try to save her, but the surgeon came out of the operating room and shook his head. "I'm afraid we are going to lose her," he told Alex, my brother-in-law. "We are working against time."

It was midnight in Chattanooga, but I ran up to the hospital rooftop and called Pe. "We are going to lose Gail."

He prayed quietly and said, "With God, nothing is impossible."

I ran down, took Chicky's and Alex's hands, and right there in the crowded room, I prayed, "Lord, I am not asking for Gail's physical life, but I am asking for her spiritual life. Please show Yourself strong on Your own behalf so that others might come to know You."

Gail survived. But one of her vocal cords had been cut during the surgery. I went in to see her. She was crying. "I want to die." Her raspy voice was barely above a whisper.

I held her hand. "Gail, *God* just brought you through. You *have to* live."

A staunch Buddhist for whom I had prayed for twenty years, she said brokenly, "I want to find Jesus."

Tears streaming down my face, I grasped her hand, "Talk to Him now. He loves you just as you are. Ask Jesus to forgive you of your sins and become your Savior."

What a glorious moment for me as she received my Jesus! I stayed with her for four months in Australia, nursed her to recovery, and found a Bible-believing church for her. She lived another ten years with no voice, but she still opened her home for Bible study, and until the day God took her home, she was an encouragement and strength to the people in her church.

During this time, my office manager could not handle the many hats I wore, so she hired four more staff to help and even contracted an accountant and a medical consultant to help her over the hump until I got back. I was grateful that I could nurse Gail back to health, but I knew I would have a backlog of work on my return.

Unshackled

Back at home, life was still a treadmill of busyness because I had never learned to say no. But now I was learning that I could get on and off the treadmill. God had to bring me to the place where all that had consumed my time had to be put on hold. I finally fell to my knees because everything had become out of my control.

I had to come to the realization that there was nothing I could have done about Pe's cancer or about Gail's near death except to seek Him for whom my soul had so longed.

In desperation, I had asked the Lord to answer me when I had no answers. In my deepest, darkest, unable-to-see places, I had asked Him to save them when I could do nothing to save either of them. When I had let go of my sweet Pe, God gave him back to me. When I had given away Gail and prayed for her spiritual life instead, God gave her back to us *and* brought her to Himself.

I was unshackled and set free by those moments of desperate dependency. I was back on God's path instead of my own. In my surrender, God opened another Red Sea Road by parting the waters and drew me back to Himself.

In my surrender to Him, I learned to say *no* to the things that would eventually become "wood, hay, and stubble" and *yes* to eternal treasures that would not be corrupted and were safe, where thieves could not break in and steal them. And this was where the Holy Spirit sharpened my gifts.

I found myself sharing more of the Scripture verses I had memorized. My gift of encouragement slipped into the lives of so many who were searching. My heart was drawn closer to the One who had called me to be His own. When people wanted me to counsel and pray with them, my motto changed from "I have no time" to "It is not an interruption. It is God-ordained." I was more at peace with myself.

Seeing With Spiritual Eyes

More challenges came, and they put me back onto a roller coaster. On February 21, 2003, my beautiful twin grandbabies were born in Greer, South Carolina. They were only a little over three pounds each, and it was my privilege as their grandmother to help take care of them. I wanted to help Zaw's family in any way I could, and I placed this as a high priority.

They became our joy and delight—two precious baby girls who brought so much happiness into our lives.

March 4, 2003, marked our thirty-sixth wedding anniversary, and Pe whisked me away to our chalet in Gatlinburg for a three-day reprieve. When that brief time was nearly over, I held him tight, not wanting him to leave.

At this time, I was still writing my Bible study, *Acts: Empowered for Jesus*, alongside teaching the lessons that went with it every Wednesday. In my absence, several of the ladies whom I called my "Timothys" were able to lead my class, and I believe this allowed them to grow and mature in their faith because they have since moved forward in training their own "Timothys" to share God's Word with boldness.

I was also able to oversee Pe's practice long distance. At the same time, the added responsibility I entrusted to my office manager to see us through this time allowed her to develop many administrative qualities, giving her much-needed confidence.

I missed being with Pe, but I knew I was where I needed to be. He had always been gracious in taking care of our home and himself while I had to be away. I knew he missed me, but for such a time as this, he encouraged me to stay where I was. "Enjoy each moment, Darling. Make memories of each one. Moments will pass, but the memories we have made will be forever in our hearts."

Looking back, I am grateful I did. It was a special bonding time as I held and cared for these babies, who had grabbed hold of my heart. It gave me such peace as I soothed them to sleep or played with them when they were awake.

Then, the Lord gave me a special gift that thrilled my heart. I was missing Pe more than usual as it was my birthday, and he was not there to celebrate it with me. The tiny babies and I were in my study bedroom. As usual, I sat them up in their little cocoon chairs with towels rolled up snuggly on each side so they could lean back safely while I worked and watched them at the same time.

I heard cooing noises, causing me to glance over. That's when I saw them staring at each other for the first time. Amazed, I suddenly realized they had become aware of each other at that precise moment. If I had not been there, I would have missed that heart-stopping experience.

God had provided this precious moment to show me that though I felt far away from Him, He was near and had never left me. It was not about the time I did not have with Him, but rather about my oblivion of not recognizing that His presence was always with me every moment.

"O Lord Jesus, open my eyes and let me see with Your eyes." My tears flowed as I dropped a kiss on each plump little cheek.

I could almost hear Pe's gentle voice as if he were here holding my hand and looking into my eyes. *When we have grateful hearts, we don't have room for complaints or grumbling. Our soul is satisfied, and our minds are at peace when we see with spirit eyes.*

Lord Jesus, thank You for the miracles You shower me with each precious moment. Help me to see with Your eyes!

Chapter 40

Come Take a Moment with Me

Come walk with me, along the golden sands.
A single set of footprints always needs a helping hand.
–Alice Morris[1]

Lord, You told me when I decided to follow You,
You would walk and talk with me all the way.
But I'm aware that during the most troublesome times of my life
there is only one set of footprints.
I just don't understand why, when I need You most, You leave me.[2]

On July 2, 2003, Zaw transferred his family to Chattanooga, and we were overjoyed when they moved in with us while they built their new home just six minutes away. Zaw found a position as an internal medicine specialist and worked as a hospitalist in Cleveland, Tennessee, about thirty minutes from our house. They stayed with us for about a year. It was an affectionate time of bonding with the babies as we watched them grow month after month. Those are times that we will always hold to our hearts.

I had picked up where I had left off at home, only the piles had stacked higher, and work had more issues to take care of. I gave up my Bible teaching for a sabbatical as I tried to tackle the most urgent tasks and let go of the ones that could wait a little longer. I stepped away several times a day to take time for what was important and made myself step in and work on the tasks that needed to be done first. I stacked the rest into piles in order of their urgency and, bit by bit, kept my head above water even when more work came in, leaving me feeling overwhelmed.

Pe would hold me close and remind me, "Jesus is holding out His hands to you and inviting you to take a moment and rest in Him."

I taped a note to the edge of my computer screen: "Taking care of myself is not self-indulgence; it is self-preservation. If I am empty, I have nothing to give others." Those few words of wisdom helped me not to feel guilty when I was not working nonstop. I took time to encourage and strengthen others as I listened to their hearts.

"Darling," Pe said, "you have a stack of cards that came in the mail. They are from the people you sent letters to. I am sure their spirits were uplifted by what you wrote. I get so many people telling me what your notes and letters mean to them." He gave me a squeeze. "I don't know how you find the time to do what you are doing."

His sweet words meant the world to me. "I'm learning to redeem my time, Sweetheart. Where I used to feel I had no time, now I spend the first half hour in the morning letting the Word of God speak to me. I know firsthand now that He loves me with a love that will never let me go, and I know that every detail of my life is important to Him. I drown myself in the Scriptures instead of letting my circumstances drown me."

He put his cheek next to mine, "I love you so much, Darling. You are the dearest thing on earth to me. You are my soulmate and my perfect companion."

"And you are to me. My forever husband and sweetheart."

Many others loved him too. Through care, generosity, and prayer, Pe loved each one of his patients, and they loved him. The *Chattanooga Times* even listed him among the thirty-three most loved, respected, and well-known people in the city.

There was a special light about him because he lived in complete obedience as a child of God; everyone who met Pe was drawn to him. This man was a highly educated professional at the top of his field who had achieved every human measure of success. And all the while, he was unshakably humble and gentle. And he always maintained a decidedly simple faith and complete trust in his heavenly Father, who abundantly loved him and held him in His hands.

Through Pe's guidance, I had learned to look into the eyes of Jesus. I no longer looked at the mountain in front of me. Instead, I chipped into the mountain bit by bit and felt a freedom in moving forward. It had taken me a long time to finally grasp the truth of what Pe was trying to tell me as he quoted Matthew 11:28-30 each time I felt like drowning: "Come to me, all you who are weary and burdened, and I will give you rest. Take my yoke upon you and learn from me, for I am gentle and humble in heart, and you will find rest for your souls. For my yoke is easy and my burden is light" (NIV).

I had memorized this passage. I even kept repeating it in my mind. But somehow, it never took root because surrendering my burdens was not a habit in my life. I felt I had to carry my burden, no matter how heavy it got. This was what I was taught growing up, and it had become my way of life. It was not until I stopped to take the opportunity Jesus was offering me, until I was willing to spend a moment with Him, to come to Him and learn from Him, that I looked into His face and finally saw myself as He saw me, carrying the weight of the heavy burdens I had placed on myself, struggling to lift them up only to find myself bowed over in a vain attempt to do everything on my own.

I felt weighed down by my burdens, but I also felt the longing for rest that only Jesus can give. I had to stretch up and give Jesus my burden. It was too heavy. I had to let go of it—to lay it down. I saw the beauty of this verse in the word *my*. It was as if Jesus were saying, "You are under a yoke that makes you weary. Shake it off. Give it to me and take *My* yoke instead. *My* yoke is easy, and *My* burden is light."

With the realization that dawned on me, a word picture came to my mind: all I had to

do was take the offer to yoke up with Jesus. In that moment, I figured if I yoked myself to Him, I would be lifted off my feet because He was stronger and bigger, and He would be the one pulling the burden—a comical picture perhaps, but I found rest for my soul.

Oh, how freeing it was to finally let go of the guilt, stress, and agitation that comes from not letting go. I was free at last from trying to perform, trying to please everyone, and trying to take responsibility for everyone and everything that was not mine to take. There is a song by Larnelle Harris that I often repeat to help me remember. I learned through his song that I had to trust God; trying my very best would not get me anywhere. I was running in circles without being able to rest. I had been worrying and fretting but had not taken the time to pray. It made me come to the realization that I could do nothing in my own strength. It had to come from the Lord.

I had found the rest that Jesus, the Good Shepherd, had already provided, the strength that Jehovah God promises to all who will come.

"Come," God's prophet Isaiah had called out. Like the children of Israel, where before I had not eyes to see nor ears to hear, I finally understood what this call from God means. It is an invitation to come and be *soul-satisfied*: "Come, all you who are thirsty, come to the waters; and you who have no money, come, buy and eat! Come, buy wine and milk without money and without cost. Why spend money on what is not bread, and your labor on what does not satisfy? Listen, listen to me, and eat what is good, and your soul will delight in the richest of fare" (Isaiah 55:1–2 NIV).

Jesus said of Himself, "Whoever drinks the water I give them will never thirst. Indeed, the water I give them will become in them a spring of water welling up to eternal life" (John 4:14 NIV).

"On the last and greatest day of the festival, Jesus stood and said in a loud voice, 'Let anyone who is thirsty come to me and drink. Whoever believes in me, as Scripture has said, rivers of living water will flow from within them'" (John 7:37–38 NIV).

Jesus offers this wonderful gift for anyone who will come to Him. He will take over every burden and will Himself carry the burden bearer on His strong shoulders. He has promised.

Chapter 41

My Strength, My Shield, and My Strong Tower

On the day of trouble He will conceal me in His tabernacle;
He will hide me in the secret place of His tent;
He will lift me up on a rock.
And now my head will be lifted up above my enemies around me,
and I will offer sacrifices in His tent with shouts of joy;
I will sing, yes, I will sing praises to the LORD.
–Psalm 27:5–6 NASB

He whispered, "My precious child, I love you
and will never leave you, never, ever, during your trials and testings.
When you saw only one set of footprints, it was then that I carried you."[1]

Our home was a haven for our family. Zaw and his family often came over to enjoy Pe's Burmese curries and his flavorful rice dishes, and Mimi would often drive up to Chattanooga from Atlanta.

We kept our twin granddaughters over the weekends. They loved playing pretend with their Pho Pho and Grammy. We would walk into their bedroom while Pe made the sound of a make-believe car driving up to their make-believe restaurant. The four of us would have tea parties in the living room with my Royal Doulton China tea set, feasting on cucumber sandwiches and scones and drinking cranberry tea.

Every weekend the girls stayed with us, Pe and I would sleep in the master bedroom downstairs on the not-so-comfortable blow-up mattress next to the girls' twin beds. We had cozy times together, reading their favorite bedtime stories before they drifted off to sleep. Some mornings I would wake up to see them in the kitchen with their Pho Pho, making an elaborate fruit plate heaped with summer fruit.

I kept Pe's words close to my heart. *Enjoy each moment, Darling. Make precious memories. Moments don't last, but we will have those memories forever.*

Then, depths of sorrow upon sorrow came in waves.

Seven-Hour Shifts

"Tita, Mummy has lung cancer, and the doctors don't expect her to live. She is at home now. Daddy is in the hospital. He suffered a heart attack and fell over on the busy highway as he was crossing the road to get to the pharmacist."

It was 2005, and I went back to Australia. As my parents' final days came to a close, I remained off and on in Australia to help nurse my mother and my Daddy at the same time. For almost two years, I flew back and forth far across half the world, often separated from my husband and children.

My father suffered several heart attacks and was diagnosed with dementia. It was sad to watch both of them slowly decline before my eyes. They wanted to remain at home, and Gail, Chicky, and I nursed them in seven-hour shifts—sponge baths, toilet, feeding, dressing, and medications. Nurses came to check on them and taught us how to give morphine injections to Mummy, who was in the last stages of metastatic lung cancer.

After my shifts through the night, as soon as it was daylight, I would shower, put on my sneakers, warmup pants, and jacket, cover my head with my hoodie, and head toward the promenade walks along the beach. Time stood still for me as I walked, jogged, or meandered in the parks along the seashore during my off-duty time. The crashing of the ocean waves, the white seagulls squawking, and the whistling of the rushing wind was a balm to my tired body and soul. At these times, I would belt out my favorite praise songs and shout aloud my prayers to my all-seeing, all-loving heavenly Father.

With a sixteen-hour time difference between Pe and me, I would find a bench facing the ocean and wait for him to call. "Darling," he might say, "I miss you so much. It's 10 p.m. here, and I'm in bed holding the photograph you gave me when you were sixteen. You were beautiful then, but you are much more beautiful to me now. I love you with all my heart."

"I love you too, Darling. I wish you could be with me, but I know you must take care of the patients. I will come home as soon as I can."

Every time we spoke, I would stare out at the ocean and imagine being there with him at our home in Chattanooga beyond the expanse of the deep blue-green ocean. It was always hard to whisper goodbye.

You Are Too Much

Despite Mummy being a Christian, it seemed my bold Christianity had become unwelcome in the house. Respecting this wish, I would pray silently at her bedside and, at her request, read her Bible to her as her vision started to decline.

All the while, my heart was crying as tears filled my eyes, and I silently prayed. *Lord Jesus, lead me to the passages in Your Word that will minister to her hurting heart. Help me to shine Your light in her darkness. I know she loves You and knows that at her journey's end, You will be there to meet her.*

As I sponge-bathed her, rubbed lotion over her thin, little body, and wrapped her with the extra towels straight from the dryer, she accepted my tender care, and her face expressed joy at my presence, which deeply comforted me. Her cancer had spread and was all throughout her. I learned to administer morphine to ease her pain.

Look Beyond the Darkness

After several months of the intensive care we were giving on a twenty-four-hour schedule, Chicky said, "We will have to have a private nurse for Daddy as we cannot manage to look after them both. It will make our load easier."

We welcomed the reprieve from the Burmese nurse we hired. But, thinking she would please Daddy, the nurse brought in an offering to appease the Hindu god that his mother had worshipped and was his family heritage.

Immediately, I felt an air of the spirit world that had haunted me through my childhood. Coupled with being told to hide my belief, the fruit basket offering she placed in Daddy's room in front of the statue of his Buddha caused a strange heaviness in my heart. *O, sweet Jesus, You seem so far away. Help me know that You are close. Let me feel Your presence. Shine Your light in this darkness.*

Pe called me from Chattanooga that night. It was a Sunday, and he was getting ready for church. I said, "Darling, I feel an oppression so strong in my spirit. It's almost as though I must suppress my Christian joy. I am so afraid."

"Don't forget that you are God's child, my Darling. Jesus has already won the victory for you, and you have nothing to fear."

He gently reminded me from 1 John 4:4–5 NIV, "You, dear children, are from God and have overcome them, because the one who is in you is greater than the one who is in the world. They are from the world and therefore speak from the viewpoint of the world, and the world listens to them."

My heart softly repeated God's Word as we got off the phone. I felt comforted as God's love enfolded me. Fear no longer held me captive because *perfect love casts out fear, for fear has torment* (from 1 John 4:18). It no longer had the power to hold me in bondage as it had done in my childhood and teen years and even into my young adult life—because God's perfect love had drawn me with an everlasting love and never let me go.

A sense of freedom washed over me, and I started singing the old hymns we had sung as children at the Methodist English High School. My cousin, Alexandria Manook, who had come to spend some time with her dying aunt, joined in. Soon, our little home hospital was filled with light and laughter and joy.

Daddy was now in a wheelchair, and every night after his nurse showered him, I would tuck him into bed. I would lean over his hospital bed rails, and as I put my cheek to his, I would see the statue of Buddha with the evening offering just above Daddy's headboard and sing "It Is Well with My Soul" until his mouth curved into a peaceful smile.

The Silver Cord

I finally had to return home again, but God, in His loving kindness, allowed me to get back to Australia in 2007, not only in time to see Mummy before she passed but giving me a moment with her as He miraculously woke her up from her coma.

"I came back, Mummy, just as I promised, to hold your hand and walk with you until it is time for you to leave me."

Her eyes flew open, and she mouthed the words, *I love you*. I had never seen a smile so radiant. She seemed as though she could see Jesus waiting for her.

I sat at her bedside and started to sing an old hymn that she and I both loved. She would often tell me in those last suffering moments that someday, the silver cord that held her here would break and that she wouldn't be singing the same songs that we would sing together. She spoke of the day when she would wake up with joy to find herself in the palace of the King and see Jesus face to face. How apt that the beloved song she sang ends with "saved by grace," which was her middle name![2] As she slowly drew her last breath, Evelyn Grace was ushered into the arms of her Savior.

Chapter 42

The Vine Dresser

Thou hast formed us for Thyself,
and our hearts are restless until they find rest in Thee.
—Saint Augustine[1]

"I am the vine; you are the branches.
If you remain in me and I in you, you will bear much fruit;
apart from me you can do nothing."
—John 15:5 NIV

On my return home after Mummy's celebration service, we discovered that Pe had developed a second cancer.

Daddy's dementia became more severe, and not long after that, he followed Mummy, but I was unable to say goodbye to him. My Jesus became for me a constant companion. At times I could hardly go on, and it was then that I felt the Lord's gentle arms holding me. I rested in that sweet fellowship.

Pe was put on chemotherapy to shrink the lymphoma cells. Although the oncologist said he still had several years to live, with the onset of the second cancer, his chemotherapy treatments prevented him from continuing to see patients.

"Dr. Tin, I know you have been keeping your regular schedule with doing surgery and seeing patients. But you cannot work for at least six months because I will have to give you strong doses of several chemotherapy drugs that will knock you out. We will start today."

"May I have a week to take care of his schedule?" I ventured.

"No, Mrs. Tin, you cannot have a week; we must start today."

What followed was an intense amount of scrambling. I spent my days running back and forth between Pe and work. I would sit beside and nurse my dear husband during his eight-hour-long infusions and then try, most of the time unsuccessfully, to get replacement physicians for both the Chattanooga and North Georgia practice locations.

Canceling patients' appointments and surgeries, coding for the one replacement physician I could hire, and making sure the office staff was looked after while sitting with charts at Pe's bedside as he went through intensive care was a small nightmare.

After that came week after week of chemotherapy and dealing with everything that is involved with an intensive, aggressive six-month treatment. Pe was in and out of hospitals with white blood count loss, anemia, pneumonia, exhaustion, loss of weight, hair, muscle, and immunity. This was his life and mine, and I had to learn to take one day at a time.

During these heartbreaking moments, all I wanted to do was to hide in the safe and secure haven of my heavenly Father's arms. But my responsibilities were heavy on me as I tried to keep the practice afloat. I had to keep moving.

I was by Pe's side, taking care of him twenty-four-seven, and while he was having the transfusions, I sat by his side and worked doggedly on a mountain of charts, papers, and telephone messages that I carried back and forth between home, hospital, and clinic.

My quiet moments only came when I was driving Pe. As he sat exhausted or asleep after each aggressive session, I would cry out to the Lord in my aloneness, "I don't know the way, but You do, Lord. I can't see around the corner, but You can. I don't know the answer, but You have everything under control. I am out of control, so please help me, Lord Jesus, help me carry on."

I was struck by the words from Psalm 119:105–107 in a different translation from the ones I was used to: "By your words I can see where I'm going; they throw a beam of light on my dark path. I've committed myself and I'll never turn back from living by your righteous order. Everything's falling apart on me, GOD; put me together again with your Word" (MSG).

As Pe always reminded me, "God's Word is a lamp unto our feet, a light unto our path. But sometimes, He shines His lamp just at our feet, not His light for the whole way, so we will learn to trust Him. The more we read God's Word, the more we will know Him, grow closer to Him, and trust Him more. The more we give Him our heart, the stronger our love for Him will grow."

How true.

May I Have This Cushion?

Pe's sister Patricia came to see him. "Son Son, how can you be so calm?" She was beside herself and was crying at the thought of what her baby brother was going through.

"Ma Ma, it is all right. The Lord is taking care of me, and I don't have to worry about what the next day will be like." He opened his Bible to Deuteronomy 31:8 9 (NIV) and read aloud: "The Lord himself goes before you and will be with you; He will never leave you nor forsake you. Do not be afraid; do not be discouraged."

He patted the seat next to him on the sofa. "Don't be afraid; I am not. When it is time for Jesus to take me home, He will."

Her husband, Roy, was holding my favorite—and worn—cushion on which was embroidered "For God so loved the world that He gave His one and only Son, that whoever believes in Him shall not perish but have everlasting life. John 3:16."

He looked at me. "Nita, do you think I could have a cushion like this?"

"Of course, Roy, you can take that cushion home."

Roy loved Pe. Was it because of Pe's cancer that death could have become a reality in Roy's mind? Had the words *have everlasting life* and *not perish* become more attractive because he didn't know what his end would be? I could not tell. Soon after our first arrival in New York, Ron had declared that he was an atheist. But now, the Lord allowed me to share my salvation experience with him. Our joy became ten-fold near the end of Roy's life as he seemed at peace when Pe and I prayed with him.

Pray for Me in Burmese

"Six months," the oncologist had said. But amazingly, Pe went back to work at his practice after just *three* months. The weekly infusions contin-ued, and I gave him Fridays off so he could recover over the weekend. He was in top form.

Pe always had the oncology nurses in stitches. He would choose the chair next to the window where the snacks were and say, "I love coming here. I can catch up on my beauty sleep."

To the oncologist, he joked, "As long as I keep my hair, I'm okay."

To which Dr. C. would laughingly say, "Dr. Tin, I will pray for your cancer. Maybe you will keep your hair."

No matter what he went through, Pe was always positive and happy. He was back to working full-time and still enjoyed cooking and taking care of the garden and the swimming pool.

A month after Pe had returned to work, Chicky called. "Tita, Gail has had a massive brain hemorrhage."

Pe and I, along with Mimi and Zaw's family, went to spend the last Christmas with her while she was in intensive care.

Three weeks later, I was back home and scheduled to speak at church the following night. I was on my way to the ladies' gathering when Chicky called. "We are sitting with Gail in the intensive ward," she said. "Gail is slowly fading. I will keep you posted." I could not keep my phone on, so I told Chicky to call the house, and Pe took the call.

That evening, at the exact moment I shared with the ladies that my little sister Gail was probably stepping into heaven taking deep breaths of the new and celestial air and finding God's hand reaching out to her, she woke up in glory and stepped into her Savior's waiting arms.

I flew to Sydney the following day and met with the pastor to arrange her celebration service. It was God-glorifying, and many in the church shared how her life had touched and encouraged them even though she had no voice due to her cut vocal cord. God had given her ten more years of life so she could make an impact for the kingdom.

Then Chicky's aggressive bladder cancer also returned on the day we said goodbye to Gail, and she was now suffering from repeat surgeries, radiation, and chemotherapy. I went to be with her at the onset but left after a few weeks as I could not leave Pe for long.

Amazingly, as my husband and Chicky went through their intensive cancer treatments at about the same time, my little sister, a Buddhist, called Pe almost every other day from Australia, asking him to pray in Burmese for her. And in God's wonderful timing, she prayed to receive Christ as he prayed with her.

My sweet Pe said, "God gave me my cancer so Chicky could know Jesus as her Savior."

Spiritual Treasures

A year and one month after Gail went home, Chicky finally succumbed to her cancer. To see them each suffer for almost a year and shrink to skin and bone was heartbreaking and more than I could take. But joy filled my heart that they both received Jesus as their Savior and were in heaven with Him.

The pain of their passing, along with all Pe had to suffer, split my world apart. Yet I learned through the things God had brought me through that when I could no longer carry on, He hid me in the secret depths of His tabernacle.

God had moved me from a life shackled by darkness, doubt, and despair to a free, full, and overflowing life. He has become my strength, my shield, my buckler, and my strong tower. He fights my battles for me as I lean on Him.

Looking back now, I can trace the steps where my heavenly Father had pursued me with infinite love—and the exact moment I became aware of His everlasting love when He finally drew me to Himself.

I discovered two treasures that I would not exchange for anything this world has to offer: First were the valuable lessons I gleaned as, moment by moment, I learned to rest in His strong arms during the lowest ebbs of my life. Second was the dramatic discovery of my hiding place, where I ultimately found the peace for which I had so desperately searched.

God continues to weave a tapestry of silver and dark thread in my life as He draws me closer to Himself. But I have learned that the unhappy dark threads are as necessary as the happy silver ones and that the master Weaver knows what He is doing as He skillfully works.

Chapter 43

A New Song in My Mouth

He put a new song in my mouth,
a hymn of praise to our God.
Many will see and fear the LORD
and put their trust in him
–Psalm 40:3 NIV

We continued hosting our friends and family, taking care of our patients, traveling together on delightful cruises and to far-away romantic
places, and leading a wonderful and beautiful life entwined with each
other. But the shadow of cancer always loomed over our heads.

Pe has always had his mind prepared for going home, even while present and active in life. His heart never misses a beat as he willingly gives
of himself to all whom God brings into his path.

"With cancer, you never know when. We just have to thank the Lord
for the time He has given me. Patients ask me when I am going to retire,
and I always tell them, 'Moses never retired. I am working for the Lord
and will work until the Lord takes me home."

I cradled Pe's head. "I thank the Lord every day for giving me you. I cannot think of the day when we are no longer walking side by side, holding each other's hand."

Through it all, God became nearer and dearer as He alone became our strength and solace, our shield and strong tower. We memorized Psalm 27 together.

We had walked through his three cancers, through my mother's lung cancer and Chicky's bladder cancer, through my father's heart disease and dementia, and I had watched my two little sisters die thirteen months apart from each other.

As I hid in the secret depths of Jesus' loving arms, He became my hiding place. When I could go on no longer, He would hold me up, and all I could do was seek His face. As I fought each battle, He placed me high above my circumstances, and I offered Him sacrifices of praise.

God had to bring me back to the path of molding me into the image of Jesus. As the master Potter, He put me in the refiner's fire, burning the dross, the grime, the strife, and everything that would keep His image from being formed in my life. What were the riches He poured into my empty hands when my life was at its lowest ebb? It was Himself.

When He lifted me up out of the miry pit, it was to put me on a platform to be a trophy of His splendor. When He put a new song in my mouth, it was to bring others to Him. My speaking engagements down through the years had all been orchestrated by Him.

I thought of the story of a nightingale with a broken wing that sang sweet notes even in her pain. *God would not waste my pain.* His purpose was that through the pain, I would be able to encourage and strengthen others. What message could I bring if I, as the messenger, had no understanding?

Only through the cracks can a broken jar reveal the light it holds inside. The more the brokenness, the greater the light will shine.

God Has Everything to Say

I was at a women's retreat in Gatlinburg, Tennessee, for a combined gathering of six churches from the Chattanooga area. I had been asked to be the lead speaker for a group of women who met yearly to encourage, uplift, and strengthen women of all ages.

As I reached the steps leading to the podium, I suddenly had stage fright as my mind went back to a few days after 9/11 when I was invited to speak at a church. As I pulled in, the parking lot was full, and more cars circled around. I did find a place to park but stayed sitting in the car. What was happening? I had been told there would only be about three hundred women in attendance. I called Pe. "I'm feeling scared. I just want to stay in the car. There are a lot of women going into the church, and I have nothing to say."

"God has everything to say. Just go in, Darling. Jesus has already gone before you."

The event had been moved to the church auditorium from the banquet hall because of the crowd. Three hundred more women, shaken by the 9/11 tragedy, had come to hear the message.

I forced my mind back to the present conference. There was a hush. The retreat coordinator stepped up to open the last session, announcing me as the closing speaker. Strengthened by what the Lord had done for me so many times previously, I walked to the podium and looked out at the ladies, but my knees started knocking as I silently prayed, *I'm not ready, Lord, I'm not. Please help me.*

I had no time to collect my thoughts. They turned on my microphone. I heard Pe's voice encouraging me, and I felt the Lord leading me to share my own experience of God becoming my hiding place in my valley of despair.

But how do I get His message across? Lord, empty me of me that I might be filled with You.

The Holy Spirit took over as I recounted how the Lord had used sorrow in my life to lead me to the place where only He mattered—the message I want to share with anyone who will listen or read. "I did not know then that God was not finished with me yet—and that time and time again, I would be placed in the refiner's fire, where impurities are burned away in the scorching heat. Much like the goldsmith who finally sees his reflection in the gold, silver, or bronze pieces as the dross burns away, and the potter who is finally satisfied as he removes his masterpiece from the fire—God is still in the process of working on me."

I looked at their faces.

"I learned through the storms and the valleys of my life that in just such a way, God takes my ugliness and turns it into beauty, and He takes my weakness and converts it into strength. Yes, I was one of those transported from my usual habitat. With the result of being carried away, God, in His sovereign and everlasting love, was ever drawing me to Himself with loving kindness as He took me through the refiner's fire to remove everything that would keep me from loving Him with all my heart, soul, mind, and strength. Until Jesus takes me home, I remain the clay in the Master Potter's hand. And He is not finished with me yet."

Quietly I prayed, *Help me to finish well, Lord. May this evening bring glory and honor to you alone.*

"God is writing His story, and we get to become a part of it. Nothing is wasted. We have the wonderful opportunity of joining Him where He is already working. Yes, you may sometimes feel that you are being pummeled. And at times, you may feel that you just can't go on. Don't give up! You are becoming a trophy of His grace, His masterpiece lighting up the dark and drawing those who sit in darkness waiting to hear His story of salvation through amazing grace."

How do I address their pain? Lord, help me to go on.

"Are you disappointed with your life? Are you discouraged because things are not turning out the way you had planned? Do you feel trapped in your past? Are you going through more than you can bear? Take heart. God can see around the corner where we cannot. We may only see the underside of the tapestry He is weaving in your life and mine, but He knows and sees the other side, which will finally have the beautiful patterns He has planned for you and me."

My heart was beating out of my chest. *Stop your hands from shaking Nita. Finish well.*

"God does care. He hears us when we call and speaks to us if we will listen. As C. S. Lewis so graphically writes in *The Problem of Pain*, 'He whispers to us in our pleasures but shouts in our pain.'[1] He lets us know He will always walk with us in our trials and suffering. He is our Jehovah *Shammah* and longs to hold us to His breast as a mother would her child. Be comforted that He knows and feels our pain because He has already gone before us. He loves us so much He died for us. So run into His outstretched arms. He is waiting for you."

I sat back in my seat. Pe was right. God had everything to say.

Chapter 44

Farewell, Nepal! God Met Me in Your Mountains

"There is a place near me where you may stand on a rock.
When my glory passes by, I will put you in a cleft in the rock
and cover you with my hand until I have passed by."
–Exodus 33:21–22 NIV

And we all, who with unveiled faces contemplate the Lord's glory,
are being transformed into his image with ever-increasing glory,
which comes from the Lord, who is the Spirit.
–2 Corinthians 3:18 NIV

February 10, 2014, Kathmandu Hotel

I had been so deep in my reverie that my mind struggled to return to our present surroundings in Nepal. We had several hours until we needed to get to the Kathmandu airport. From then, on to Mumbai, and then the long trip back home. I looked at Pe and around the bedroom suite, and ever after, the scene before me has never failed to pull at my heartstrings.

With the Bible opened on his chest as gentle snores moved it up and down and his lips gently curved into a restful, peaceful sleep, my husband was a picture of an innocent child asleep in his Father's arms. Mimi, her covers pulled over her head and totally relaxed, was fast asleep in the corner of the room where a cot had been prepared for her. These two gentle souls, so like each other in their childlike faith and trust and sweetness of soul, breathed in gentle, rhythmic cadence in beds that enveloped them like soft cocoons.

God had become a constant hope in our lives. Pe and I had weathered so many storms together. He was doing what he loved and was fulfilling his call as a healer. He was strong and competent as a physician, and no cancer had overcome his attitude and joy in living. He worked circles around his staff, loved his patients, and continued with his innovative, cutting-edge eye surgeries. He loved his home, his life, and his God.

Sleep eluded me. My heart was so full of joy and thankfulness that I could not contain it. I wanted to shout out loud. My grateful heart knew no bounds as I gave thanks to my God, who, in His everlasting love for this Burmese Buddhist girl, had drawn me to Himself.

I knew what I needed to do. Coming to Nepal and seeing the culture I had come from reminded me of God's calling on my life to share His story. The new song God had put in my heart was a never-ending, full to overflowing with gratitude and praise for Him. Yes, many needed to hear it! Why had I been wasting all this time? I got down on my knees next to the bed and then sat on the couch by the window.

Pe woke up, kissed my forehead, and sat close to me. "Good morning, Darling. You're up early."

I rested my head on his shoulder. "I had so much to process in my head. I'm so glad God brought us to Kathmandu."

Forever etched in my memory since I left Nepal is the wonderment and awe of a God who raised up people of Hindu and Buddhist cultures, calling them to be church planters to bring many more souls into His kingdom.

And for me, the trip kindled some of the fire that had died down. God ignited my focus to fulfill the plan He had for me.

Chapter 45

Beauty for Ashes

...to bestow on them a crown of beauty instead of ashes,
the oil of joy instead of mourning,
and a garment of praise instead of spirit of despair.
They will be called oaks of righteousness,
a planting of the Lord, for the display of his splendor.
–Isaiah 61:3b NIV

When we returned from our trip, we settled back into life as usual until a huge shift threw us into God's arms again. On November 28, 2016, the night of the Gatlinburg wildfires, we received a call from Sentry Alarms that our chalet had burned to ashes in the fire. We had just returned home a little earlier than planned and would otherwise have been in the fire.

We stood at the foot of the blackened ruins of our once-beautiful mountain retreat. All that remained was part of the stone chimney. The whole building had blown up in the fierce wind and roaring fires. Our three-bedroom rental cabin just minutes away also burned to the ground.

Pe held me close to him. "Let's thank the Lord that He kept us safe. We need to pray for those who might not have gotten away safely."

This chalet was where we'd had ladies' retreats and family get-togethers, and it was where my Pe and I could be by ourselves. It was here that God met me in the mountains, here that my study guide *Acts: Empowered to Live for Jesus* was birthed, and here that I would sing at the top of my lungs to the God of the Universe and be motivated and energized.

It was here where we had kept all our family heirlooms, the treasures—with all the memories they held—that I had brought from Australia after my parents and my two little sisters had passed. Pe wiped the tears from my face with his kisses.

Jesus held us close in the sanctuary of His heart and filled us with joy and peace as we began to rebuild. Mimi worked with the architect and the builder, and out of the ashes, a new chalet began to rise.

"See, Darling?" Pe said. "God promised in His Word to give us beauty for ashes. And He is doing it!"

Hard as it may sometimes be, I rest in the thought that, as a potter turns up the kiln's temperature just enough to burn away impurities, God does the same for us in the heat of our trials, allowing beautiful patterns to emerge. As our weaknesses shrink away, we are left firmer and stronger. We can arise with each new day and trust God to make our lives into something beautiful, something good.

This Is Not Our Home

We know God's purpose is to conform us to Jesus Christ, but we do not always understand the methods He uses in our lives. We do not always understand the periods of waiting He requires of us. But by seeing ourselves as clay and recognizing we are in the hands of a wise and knowing Master Potter, we can be confident of the process.

He is not careless. He wants the best for us. He knows what He is doing and understands better than we do the molding and preparation we each need. He takes great care with us, His earthen vessels, but He always waits for our response. And in the measure that we respond to His leading, He continues working His higher plans for us.

In the depths of the darkness, I would cry: "Will there be a reprieve? What are you doing, God? Hold me! I don't know where to hide." I found my shelter and hiding place in 2 Corinthians 4:6–18 (NIV).

For God, who said, "Let light shine out of darkness," made his light shine in our hearts to give us the light of the knowledge of God's glory displayed in the face of Christ.
But we have this treasure in jars of clay to show that this all-surpassing power is from God and not from us. We are hard pressed on every side, but not crushed; perplexed, but not in despair; persecuted, but not abandoned; struck down, but not destroyed. We always carry around in our body the death of Jesus, so that the life of Jesus may also be revealed in our body. For we who are alive are always being given over to death for Jesus' sake, so that his life may also be revealed in our mortal body. So then, death is at work in us, but life is at work in you. It is written: "I believed; therefore I have spoken." Since we have that same spirit of faith, we also believe and therefore speak, because we know that the one who raised the Lord Jesus from the dead will also raise us with Jesus and present us with you to himself. All this is for your benefit, so that the grace that

is reaching more and more people may cause thanksgiving to overflow to the glory of God.

I had to see the invisible, as the passage continues,

Therefore we do not lose heart. Though outwardly we are wasting away, yet inwardly we are being renewed day by day. For our light and momentary troubles are achieving for us an eternal glory that far outweighs them all. So we fix our eyes not on what is seen, but on what is unseen, since what is seen is temporary, but what is unseen is eternal.

That treasure is Jesus living in us. It is unique to humanity and available only to all who believe in Jesus. The very power of God is contained in these human bodies of clay, these earthen vessels. I not only had this treasure, but I was constantly reminded that our afflictions are for the moment and that earth is *not* our home.

I had traveled from a far country in search of *something more*. God, in His infinite wisdom, led me to Himself and continues to draw me. Oh, that wonderful attachment love of a God who would not let me go! He had been chasing me until all I could do was run to Him, where He would hold me close to His heart with unfailing love.

Chapter 46

A Victorious Celebration

They tell of the power of your awesome works—
and I will proclaim your great deeds.
They celebrate your abundant goodness
and joyfully sing of your righteousness.
–Psalm 145:6–7 NIV

Our journey in love continues and, Lord willing, will continue until one of us is taken home. It is not just an ongoing love affair but a commitment to give 100 percent to each other—a sacrificial love that puts God first and the other next—a love willing to lay down self so the other might benefit.

Yes, we have our ups and downs, and we are not always walking on roses, but we still hold hands, and our hearts still quicken at the thought of each other. He still rubs my head and neck each night, and I still massage his shoulders each morning as I pray that God will give him His strength and wisdom and guide his heart, mind, eyes, and hands—especially on the days he does surgery. We work effectively, efficiently, and productively together on patient days. His patients love and respect him. His practice is busy, and I am kept hustling.

We've made time to travel to exotic places like Italy, Spain, Madrid, Paris, Venice, and the UK, making memories, learning to tango, and celebrating our love. We've vacationed in Gatlinburg and Hawaii with our childhood friends Aye, Vic, Jenny, Ko Tu, Celina, and Gilbert, reminiscing about days gone by. Another much-loved couple, Byron and Mi Mi, joined us on our trips to Cabo. Byron and Pe had been at medical school together, and he had spent many hours at Pe's family home.

A Dream Come True

The year 2017 marked our fiftieth wedding anniversary.

Mimi called from Atlanta. "Please make sure you are in Chattanooga on March 4. I know you love to celebrate in Cabo, but we want to celebrate you. If you could wish for anything, what would you want for your special day?"

Without hesitation, I burst out, "I want a church wedding! I was a Buddhist when we got married."

Mimi designed a winter wonderland wedding. Our childhood friends, with whom we vacationed, and many relatives flew in from all over the country.

I finally had my dream fulfilled. I walked down the aisle for the first time as a child of God. Then, Pe and I repeated our marriage vows. This time, they were sacred—written by us straight from our hearts and repeated in the sight of our heavenly Father. Our church sanctuary was full of our church members and other people from far and wide who loved us.

I Am My Beloved's

As I entered the sanctuary in my white bridal dress, I felt as if I were floating on holy ground, totally feeling the presence of the Lord. My handsome husband stood beside our officiant, Pastor Eric, and as he came down the steps to offer me his arm to help me up on the platform, all my eyes could see was his beauty. Over and over in my mind was the thought, *I am my beloved's, and my beloved is mine.* My heart seemed to stand still as I put my hand in his and looked up at him. He looked back at me with so much love.

After the vows, our pastor laughingly announced that we were now "still" married. We kissed and sailed down the aisle as Jamie sang "You Raise Me Up." My twenty-two-year-old heart had wanted this. But I hadn't known at that time that a Christian wedding could not change my heart; only Jesus could.

My daughter, who orchestrated the whole wedding, turned the church gym into a winter wonderland for the reception. What more could I want? Forever closeted in my heart, soul, and mind would be this worshipful renewal of our vows.

"Darling heart," I said, "We've gone through so much pain, yet you have always filled me with joy. The light of Jesus shines in you, and it is through your life that I was drawn to Jesus. You have walked with me and shown me how to live through sorrow and happiness. My life is rich because of you, and I love you so much."

Pe pressed his cheek to mine. "You are the joy of my life, Darling. You are my Proverbs 31 wife. God gave me you because He knew I needed you."

We stopped in the hallway in front of the wall on which our favorite wooden plaque hung. It had Pe's life verse in beautiful calligraphy on its polished surface. "If serving the LORD seems undesirable to you, then choose for yourselves this day whom you will serve, whether the gods your ancestors served beyond the Euphrates, or the gods of the Amorites, in whose land you are living. But as for me and my household, we will serve the LORD" (Joshua 24:15 NIV).

Through pleasure or pain, God has been our steadfast anchor, our hope, and our joy.

Victory Cry

Three years later, we reached another celebration and another victorious milestone. March 4, 2020, was our fifty-third wedding anniversary, and God brought us full circle to give us "beauty for ashes."

We looked out from the deck of our newly rebuilt chalet in the mountains and knew that God had once again allowed a new thing. From the ashes of what we had called *Serenity Retreat* arose *Mountain Celebration*, a home that would minister to its guests. Our garden was beautifully landscaped, designed to bring joy and peace to those who came for rest, relaxation, and rejuvenation. But more importantly, our prayer continues to be that God would meet our guests wherever they are. The view is majestic and welcoming. My prayer is still, "Lord, show me your glory!" as I gaze at the undulating mountains, where mist and clouds provide a changing landscape with every gust of wind, and I can almost hear God whisper, "Seek My face."

I whisper back, "Lord, I seek Your face. Empty me of me so I can be filled with You." He has wooed me to Himself with an everlasting love, a love that will not let me go.

As Pe and I sit close together on the couch, looking at the fireplace in the great room of our new chalet, we thank God for His love for us. And we thank Him again and yet again that we are two parts of a whole who found each other and that God has given us a love without borders, a love that only longs for us to be together, where parting is difficult, and meeting again is sweet.

"I love you, my forever sweetheart." He draws me to his chest the way he did that last evening of the water festival when God first drew us to each other.

I put my head on his broad shoulders and looked up at him. "I love you too, my forever husband."

– end –

Always and forever yours!

Notes and Bibliography

Chapter 1
1. Billy Graham, Franklin Graham, Donna Lee Toney (2011). *Billy Graham in Quotes*, p.79, Thomas Nelson Inc

Chapter 2
1. Mehmet Murat Ildan, "Don't ever rule out the option of U-turn in your life, because one day you will need it! The moment you realize that you are going to the wrong direction, Turn to the right direction instantly, with a beautiful U-turn!" U Turn Quotes, Goodreads, 2023, https://www.goodreads.com/quotes/tag/u-turn.
2. "For the LORD your God is gracious and compassionate. He will not turn his face from your if you return to him." (2 Chronicles 30:9b NIV).

Chapter 3
1. C. S. Lewis, *Mere Christianity*, C.S. Lewis Pte. Ltd, 1952. New York, Harper-Collins Publishers.

Chapter 4
1. "Mandalay" is a poem by Rudyard Kipling, written and published in 1890 and first collected in *Barrack-Room Ballads, and Other Verses* in 1892. The poem is set in colonial Burma, then part of British India. "Mandalay," The Kipling Society, 2023, https://www.kiplingsociety.co.uk/poem/poems_mandalay.htm.

Chapter 5
1. Belinda Stotler, "Promises of a New Day," Family Friend Poems, 2019, https://www.familyfriendpoems.com/user/belinda-stotler-1533/.

Chapter 6
1. Oscar Wilde, quoted in Gracious Quotes, accessed July 28, 2022, https://graciousquot
es.com/memories-quotes/.

Chapter 7
1. Kevin Arnold, "The Wonder Years," recorded in Gracious Quotes, accessed July 28, 2022,
https://graciousquotes.com/memories-quotes/.

Chapter 8
1. Anonymous, quoted in Gracious Quotes, accessed July 28, 2022, https://graciousquot
es.com/memories-quotes/.

Chapter 9
1. Justin Young, "Your life is fleeting," Inspiring Quotes, accessed January 21, 2023,
https://www.inspiringquotes.us/topic/1513-fleeting/page:3.

Chapter 10
1. Aharon Appelfeld, quoted in Quote Stats, 2023, https://quotestats.com/topic/quotes
-about-searching-for-something-more/.

Chapter 11
1. Robin Wasserman, quoted in Quote Stats, 2023, https://quotestats.com/topic/quotes
-about-searching-for-something-more/.

Chapter 12
1. Carson McCullers, quoted in Goodreads, 2023, https://www.goodreads.com/author/
quotes/3506.Carson_McCullers.

Chapter 13
1. Keats, quoted in Goodreads, 2023, https://www.goodreads.com/author/quotes/
2. Nita Tin, "Darling Heart," October 16, 2000.

Chapter 14
1. Elizabeth Barrett Browning, "How Do I Love Thee" (Sonnet 43), 1850, accessed on
September 14, 2020, . Public domain.
2. Elizabeth Barret Browning, Sonnet 43.

Chapter 15
1. Lynn MacKinnon, "The Pit or the Pendulum," author's version of Edgar Allen Poe's short story "The Pit and the Pendulum," Hello Poetry, September 2014, https://hellopo etry.com/words/pendulum/.

Chapter 16
1. Rebecca Ratcliff, "'Revolution Dwells in The Heart': Myanmar's Po-ets Cut Down by the Military," Rights and Freedom Myanmar, May 16, 2021, https://www.theguardian.com/global-development/2021/may/17/revolu-tion-dwells-in-the-heart-myanmars-poets-cut-down-by-the-miltary
2. "Though I walk in the midst of trouble, you preserve my life. You stretch out your hand against the anger of my foes; with your right hand you save me," Psalm 138:7 NIV.
3. Thomas Mosie Lister, "Till The Storm Passes By" (1958), 2022, https://popularhymn s.com/till-the-storm-passes-by.

Chapter 17
1. Nita Tin, "Darling Heart," October 16, 2000.

Chapter 18
1. Rumi, "The Minute I Heard My First Love Story," Poetry Verse, accessed January 21, 2023https://www.poetryverse.com/rumi-poems/the-first-love-story.

Chapter 19
1. Henry David Thoreau, Goodreads, 2023, https://www.goodreads.com/quotes/10280 670-it-is-the-beauty-within-us-that-makes-it-possible.
2. Darren Paul Thorn, Goodreads, 2023, https://www.goodreads.com/author/quotes/1 6119263.Darren_Paul_Thorn.

Chapter 21
1. Bernie Siegel, Goodreads, 2023, https://www.goodreads.com/quotes/636786-embrac e-each-challenge-in-your-life-as-an-opportunity-for.

Chapter 22
1. Melissa McClone, Mistletoe Magic, November 21, 2013. Goodreads, 2023.

Chapter 23
1. Russell Gehrlein, "Those Whom God Uses to Heal," The Institute for Faith, Work &

Economics, March 30, 2020, https://tifwe.org/those-whom-god-uses-to-heal/. An additional quote from this source: "His power to heal can flow through you to others in very practical ways. You know the limitations of medicine that often fail to bring healing to many of these finite bodies. You know that when medicine fails, death is not the end. You can bring comfort to those who mourn. You also know that complete healing of the mind, body, and soul is ultimately found in Christ alone. Those whom God uses to heal, keep doing this great work, in His strength and for His glory."

Chapter 24
1. Edgar Albert Guest, "Trouble," Internet Poem, accessed April 6, 2022, https://internetpoem.com/edgar-albert-guest/trouble-poem/.

Chapter 25
1. Harry William Robbins, "Candy Striped Caresses," All Poetry, accessed September 14, 2022, https://allpoetry.com/poem/7230573-Candy-Striped-Caresses-by-penman.

Chapter 26
1. Jack London, Goodreads, 2023, https://www.goodreads.com/quotes/69941-life-is-not-always-a-matter-of-holding-good-cards.

Chapter 28
1. Chuck Swindoll, "Going . . . Yet Not Knowing," Insight for Living Ministries Resources, August 12, 2015, https://insight.org/resources/article-library/individual/going-yet-not-knowing.

Chapter 31
1. Martha Snell Nicholson, "Treasures." *Treasures.* Moody Press, 1952. Public domain.

Chapter 32
1. Kay Arthur, co-founded Precept Ministries International in 1970, based in Chattanooga, Tennessee. Precept is an interdenominational Christian evangelical organization whose stated mission is to engage people in relationship with God through knowing His Word, .

Chapter 33
1. Oscar Wilde, Gracious Quotes, accessed February 3, 2023, https://graciousquotes.com/contentment/.

Chapter 35
1. Henry Wadsworth Longfellow, "Kind Hearts," accessed via Goodreads, https://www.goodreads.com/quotes/783751-kind-hearts-are-the-gard ens-kind-thoughts-are-the-roots

Chapter 36
1. Langston Hughes, "The American Dream," All Poetry, accessed January 21, 2023, https://allpoetry.com/Let-America-Be-America-Again.
2. From a local magazine clipping dated 1982. The original and its citation information was lost in a flooded basement.

Chapter 38
1. Elisha Hoffman, "I Must Tell Jesus," public domain, 1894, Hymnary.org, https://hymnary.org/text/i_must_tell_jesus_all_of_my_trials.

Chapter 40
1. Alice Morris, "Come Walk with Me," February 2015, accessed March 29, 2022, https://hellopoetry.com/poem/1079505/come-walk-with-me/
2. "Footprints in the Sand," Often signed "Author Unknown," credit is sometimes given to Mary Stevenson, Margaret Fishback Powers, or Carolyn Joyce Carty, who have all registered copyrights for the poem, according to https://www.poetryfound ation.org. This version is credited to Powers, who wrote the most widely-recognized version of this poem during a time when she was "searching for direction and faced a crossroads in her life." The Crosswalk Devotional, contributing writer: Candice Lucey, April 16, 2020, www.crosswalk.com.
3. Larnell Harris, "The Strength of the Lord," LyricsMode, 2018, https://www.lyr icsmode.com/lyrics/l/larnelle_harris/the_strength_of_the_lord.html

Chapter 41
1. "Footprints in the Sand." Credited to Mary Stevenson, this 1939 copy of the poem was authenticated as genuine by a forensic specialist and said to be approximately fifty-plus years old. This would pre-date any claims made by others of authorship, including Margaret Fishback-Powers, who was said to have written it 1964, accessed March 4, 2021, footprints-in the-sand.com.
2. Fanny Crosby, "Saved by Grace," Hymnary.org, accessed January 28, 2023, https://hymnary.org/hymn/RH2011/page/389.

Chapter 42
1. St. Augustine of Hippo, *Lord, teach me to praise Thee,* "Confessions." https://www.v atican.va/spirit/documents/spirit_20020821_agostino_en.html

Chapter 43
1. C. S. Lewis, *The Problem of Pain* (New York: Macmillan, 1962, reprint, 1986), 93.

About the Author

A former Buddhist, Nita Tin is originally from Burma, currently known as Myanmar. She is the co-founder of Tin Laser Vision and was Practice Administrator of the Chattanooga and North Georgia medical practice for 45 years. She is an avid motivational speaker, a conference leader, a Bible teacher, and author. She received the 2023 Lydia Impact Award from the Scenic City Women's Network for her contribution as an Extraordinary Working Christian Woman. A movie script based on her story, *Love Without Borders*, was officially chosen by the Christian Worldview Film Festival 2023 and was awarded 2nd place. Her prolific letters of encouragement and heart-warming lectures pointing to God's grace and mercy have ministered to hundreds of students, friends, colleagues, and patients.

The journey to our eternal home is her theme, and her message is hope, strength, and encouragement for a child of God traveling through the pain and hopelessness of a fallen world and God's offer of freedom and salvation for those who are still trapped in sin's darkness. Her life's verse is found in Jeremiah 31:3. *"I have loved you with an everlasting love, Therefore with lovingkindness have I drawn you"* (AMP). God's unending love is what she pours out through her life and ministry as she seeks to draw believers closer to bask in the love of a heavenly Father. Nita describes herself as an emptied, broken vessel, saved to tell of the glorious gospel of Christ.

Made in the USA
Columbia, SC
04 April 2024

33647129R00174